Quiz Time
History

Manasvi Vohra

Published by:

V&S PUBLISHERS

F-2/16, Ansari Road, Daryaganj, New Delhi-110002
☎ 011-23240026, 011-23240027 • *Fax:* 011-23240028
Email: info@vspublishers.com • *Website:* www.vspublishers.com

Regional Office : Hyderabad
5-1-707/1, Brij Bhawan (Beside Central Bank of India Lane)
Bank Street, Koti, Hyderabad - 500 095
☎ 040-24737290
E-mail: vspublishershyd@gmail.com

Branch Office : Mumbai
Flat No. Ground Floor, Sonmegh Building
No. 51, Karel Wadi, Thakurdwar, Mumbai - 400 002
☎ 022-22098268
E-mail: vspublishersmum@gmail.com

Follow us on:

For any assistance sms **VSPUB** to **56161**
All books available at **www.vspublishers.com**

© Copyright: V&S PUBLISHERS
ISBN 978-93-815886-7-3
Edition 2014

The Copyright of this book, as well as all matter contained herein (including illustrations) rests with the Publishers. No person shall copy the name of the book, its title design, matter and illustrations in any form and in any language, totally or partially or in any distorted form. Anybody doing so shall face legal action and will be responsible for damages.

Printed at : Param Offseters, Okhla, New Delhi-110020

Publisher's Note

After the grand success of a number of Quiz Books, V&S Publishers has come out with a unique series called the *Quiz Time* containing quiz books on Mathematics, History, etc.

Quiz Time History is an exhaustive book including interesting and brainteasing questions and answers on almost all the phases of our glorious past. This quiz book consists of three main parts: Part-I, dealing with the Early and Medieval Indian History; Part-2, on the facts and figures of Modern Indian History and the Contemporary World and Part-3, containing General Questions on World History.

All the questions have been accompanied by answers to educate and enlighten the readers, *students of all ages* in general and the aspirants of *Civil Services Examinations* in particular. The Civil Services Examinations as we all know begins with the *Civil Services Aptitude Test (CSAT)*.

The **CSAT** is the new Recruitment Process of Civil Services Exams conducted by the UPSC (Union Public Service Commission). The CSAT has been brought into effect from the Civil Services Examination, 2011. This will not only enable the Government of India to choose civil servants with the right aptitudes, but also end the use of scaling system for varying subjects that has been a matter of concern for many. However, no changes have been introduced in the *Civil Services (Main) Examination* and the *Personality Test* in the scheme of *Civil Services Examination (CSE)*.

This book contains all the vital historical facts and figures which can be useful for students appearing for the above mentioned competitive examinations.

So friends, grab the book immediately and test your historical skills by solving these 1100 questions based on the various phases of Indian and World History!

Early and Medieval Indian History

Sources and Approaches to the Study of Early Indian History

Q-1. Who is known as the Father of Indian Archeology?
Ans. General Sir Alexander Cunningham

Q-2. The Rajatarangini written by Kalhana, deals with the history of which place?
Ans. Kashmir

Q-3. When was the Asiatic Society of Bengal established?
Ans. 15 January 1784

Q-4. What is epigraphy?
Ans. It is the study of inscriptions or epigraphs as writing.

Q-5. Which Greek scholar wrote a geographical treatise on the 2nd century AD India?
Ans. Ptolemy

Q-6. What is the name of Banabhatta's biography on Emperor Harshavardhana?
Ans. Harshacharita

Q-7. Which Iranian-Muslim scholar recorded his studies on India in a book called "Tarikh al-Hind" or "History of India" in the 11th century?
Ans. Al Biruni

Q-8. The study of _____ is called numismatics.
Ans. Coins

Early and Medieval Indian History

Old Indian Coins

Q-9. Who was the author of the work "Nirukta" that discussed the etymology of Vedic words?

Ans. Yaska

Q-10. Panini's "Ashtadhyayi" is a text on _____.
- Ⓐ Religion
- Ⓑ Politics
- Ⓒ Grammar
- Ⓓ Trade

Ans. Ⓒ Grammar

Q-11. Which Chola poet wrote on three successive kings: Vikrama Chola, Kulottunga II and Rajaraja II?

Ans. Ottakkuttan

Q-12. Fa-Hien's travelogue gives an account of the _____ age.
- Ⓐ Maurya
- Ⓑ Gupta
- Ⓒ Chola
- Ⓓ Mughal

Ans. Ⓑ Gupta

Q-13. How many hymns does the Rig Veda contain?

Ans. 1028

Q-14. The word "purana" means _____.
- Ⓐ New narrative
- Ⓑ Old narrative
- Ⓒ Song
- Ⓓ Verse

Ans. Ⓑ Old Narrative

Early Pastoral and Agricultural Communities The Archeological Evidence

Q-1. In the Indian subcontinent, which of the following animals was not domesticated by 9000 BCE.
- **Ⓐ** Sheep
- **Ⓑ** Goat
- **Ⓒ** Elephant
- **Ⓓ** Horse

Ans. Horse

Q-2. What was the first metal to be traded?
Ans. Copper

Q-3. Which plant did early farmers domesticate and then use for making drugs and oil?
Ans. Hemp

Q-4. Which variety of rice first appeared in the Ganges valley around 540 BC?
Ans. Wild Oryza

Q-5. What are the most of material remains of OCP culture in the form of?
Ans. Pottery

Chinese Tri-colored Pottery

Early and Medieval Indian History

Q-6. In the Iron age, which of these places have evidence of horse burials?
- **Ⓐ** Junapani
- **Ⓑ** Tekwada
- **Ⓒ** Maski
- **Ⓓ** Inamgaon

Ans. Ⓐ Junapani

Q-7. In which place did excavations provide evidence that some early communities lived in underground pits?
Ans. Kashmir

Q-8. Who were the first to use painted pottery?
Ans. Chalcolithics

Q-9. The fact that early communities believed in the Mother Goddess is evident by the discovery of female clay figurines _____ heads.
- **Ⓐ** with heads
- **Ⓑ** without heads
- **Ⓒ** with and without heads
- **Ⓓ** without limbs

Ans. Ⓒ with and without heads

Q-10. Terracotta figurines of which animal were found in the Chalcolithic levels at Kayatha?
Ans. Bulls

The Indus Valley Civilisation: Its origin, nature and decline

Q-1. The ruins of Harappa were first noticed by _____ in 1842.
- Ⓐ Charles Mason
- Ⓑ Rakhaldas Banerjee
- Ⓒ M. Wheeler
- Ⓓ Sahni

Ans. Ⓐ Charles Mason

Q-2. Which region of the Indian subcontinent was the Indus Valley civilisation located in?
- Ⓐ Northwest
- Ⓑ Northeast
- Ⓒ Southeast
- Ⓓ Southwest

Ans. Ⓐ Northwest

Q-3. The famous bronze statuette in Mohenjodaro is the _____ girl.

Ans. Dancing

Early and Medieval Indian History

Q-4. When was Mohenjodaro made a UNESCO World heritage site?
Ans. 1980

Q-5. What was the Indus Valley civilisation also known as?
Ans. Harappan civilisation.

Q-6. The Indus Valley civilisation is a _____ age civilisation.
- Ⓐ Gold
- Ⓑ Bronze
- Ⓒ Silver
- Ⓓ Copper

Ans. Ⓑ Bronze

Q-7. What are the six Harappan sites that are regarded as cities?
Ans. Harappa, Mohenjodaro, Chanhudaro, Lothal, Kalibanjan and Banwali.

Q-8. Ropar was a settlement near the _____ river.
- A: Indus
- Ⓑ Ravi
- Ⓒ Sutlej
- Ⓓ Bhogya

Ans. Ⓒ Sutlej

Q-9. What were the two main grains in the Harappan villages?
Ans. Wheat and barley

Q-10. Harappan seals were largely made out of which material?
Ans. Terracotta

Q-11. The horned God seal found in Harappa, had which of these animals at his feet?
- Ⓐ Lion
- Ⓑ Leopard
- Ⓒ Deer
- Ⓓ Wolf

Ans. Ⓒ Deer

Quiz Time History

Q-12. What are the five proposed theories for the decline of the Indus Valley civilisation?
Ans. Flood and earthquakes, Shifting of Indus, Increasing aridity, Aryan invasion and Ecological imbalance.

Q-13. The people of the Indus Valley civilisation lived in houses made of _____.
- **Ⓐ** Stone
- **Ⓑ** Hay
- **Ⓒ** Cement
- **Ⓓ** Burnt bricks

Ans. **Ⓓ** Burnt bricks

Q-14. In which Indus Valley site were camel bones discovered?
Ans. Kalibangan

Q-15. The Indus Valley script is_____.
- **Ⓐ** Dravidian
- **Ⓑ** Mesopotamian
- **Ⓒ** Undeciphered
- **Ⓓ** Persian

Ans. **Ⓒ** Undeciphered

Q-16. What does 'Mohenjodaro' mean?
Ans. Mound of the dead.

Q-17. What were Harappan stone sculptures usually made of?
Ans. Hard sandstone

Q-18. Which Indus Valley site had an artificial dockyard?
Ans. Lothal

Q-19. Which of the following grooming devices were discovered in Harappa?
- **Ⓐ** Comb
- **Ⓑ** Razor
- **Ⓒ** Nail cutter
- **Ⓓ** Scissors

Ans. **Ⓐ** Comb

Early and Medieval Indian History

Q-20. Harappan writing was largely found on _____.
- Ⓐ Walls
- Ⓑ Seals
- Ⓒ Caves
- Ⓓ Paper

Ans. Ⓑ Seals

Patterns of settlement, economy, social organisation and religion in India (c. 2000 to 500 B.C.): Archeological Perspectives

Q-1. Which animal did the Indo-Aryans first domesticate?
Ans. Horse

Q-2. How many Mahajanapadas existed?
   ⓐ 16 ⓑ 15
   ⓒ 24 ⓓ 10
Ans. ⓐ 16

Q-3. Which King who won over the ten-kings confederacy is mentioned in the Rigveda?
Ans. King Sudas

Q-4. Which two political assemblies did the Rig Vedic Aryans form to keep a check on the King's authority?
Ans. Sabha and Samiti

Q-5. In which hymn of the Rig Veda can the genesis of the caste system be found?
Ans. Purusha Sukta

Q-6. Who was the Goddess of Dawn?
Ans. Usha

Early and Medieval Indian History

Usha – the goddess of Dawn

Q-7. What were Nishkas?
Ans. A piece of metal possessing a definite weight.

Q-8. Which of these animals was used in barter economy as a unit of value?
    Ⓐ Goat   **Ⓑ Donkey**
    Ⓒ Cow   **Ⓓ Elephant**
Ans. Ⓒ Cow

Q-9. What was the head ornament worn by Aryan women?
Ans. Kurira

Q-10. What refreshing beverage made from the juice of a plant was a popular drink of the Aryans?
Ans. Soma

Evolution of North Indian Society and Culture: Evidence of Vedic texts (Samhitas to Sutras)

Q-1. How many books does the Rigveda Samhita have?
- Ⓐ 10
- Ⓑ 5
- Ⓒ 7
- Ⓓ 12

Ans. Ⓐ 10

Q-2. Name the four Vedas.
Ans. Rigveda, Yajurveda, Samaveda and Atharvaveda

Vedic texts

Q-3. What is the Sanskrit word for knowledge?
Ans. Veda

Q-4. The Aranyakas were composed by people who meditated in _____.
- Ⓐ Mountains
- Ⓑ Riversides
- Ⓒ Forests
- Ⓓ Temples

Ans. Ⓒ Forests

Early and Medieval Indian History

Q-5. The Vedanga has _____ subjects.
- **Ⓐ** 5
- **Ⓑ** 6
- **Ⓒ** 2
- **Ⓓ** 10

Ans. Ⓑ 6

Q-6. Which God does the Brahma Samhita glorify?
Ans. Lord Sri Krishna

Q-7. What is the another name for Braddha Jivakiya Tantra, a document on Ayurveda written by Sage Kashyap?
Ans. Kashyap Samhita

Q-8. What is the Pali form of the word "Sutra"?
Ans. Sutta

Q-9. Who first translated the Manusmriti into English?
Ans. Sir William Jones

Q-10. How many books is the Arthashastra divided into?
Ans. 15

Teachings of Mahavira and Buddha Contemporary Society and Early Phase of State Formation and Urbanisation

Q-1. Mahavira was the ____ Tirthankara.
- **Ⓐ** First
- **Ⓑ** Last
- **Ⓒ** Third
- **Ⓓ** Second

Ans. **Ⓑ** Last

Q-2. What does the name "Mahavira" mean?
- **Ⓐ** Great Hero
- **Ⓑ** Last Hero
- **Ⓒ** Saviour
- **Ⓓ** Believer

Ans. **Ⓐ** Great Hero

Q-3. How many great vows do Jains have in their philosophy of right-conduct?

Ans. 5

Q-4. What should a Jain who practises Asteya refrain from?
- **Ⓐ** Murder
- **Ⓑ** Stealing
- **Ⓒ** Adultering
- **Ⓓ** Lying

Ans. **Ⓑ** Stealing

Q-5. What are the two main sects within Jainism?

Ans. Digambara and Svetambara

Q-6. The monks of the Digambara sect usually wear ____ clothes.
- **Ⓐ** White
- **Ⓑ** Black
- **Ⓒ** No
- **Ⓓ** Colourful

Ans. **Ⓒ** No

Q-7. Which famous Jain text is read to lay people by monks during the festival of Paryushan?
Ans. Kalpa Sutra

Q-8. What occasion do Jains celebrate on Mahavir Jayanti?
Ans. The birth of Mahavira

Q-9. What place was marked by the UNESCO as a world heritage site and the birthplace of Gautam Buddha?
Ans. Lumbini

Statue of Gautam Buddha

Q-10. What was the name of Gautam Buddha's favourite horse?
Ans. Kanthaka

Q-11. Under what tree did Gautam Buddha attain enlightenment?
- **Ⓐ Pipal**
- **Ⓑ Neem**
- **Ⓒ Mango**
- **Ⓓ Lemon**

Ans. Ⓐ Pipal

Q-12. According to Buddhism, how many noble truths exist?
Ans. Four

Q-13. What are the Three Jewels of Buddhism?
Ans. Buddha, Dharma and Sangha

Q-14. Gautam Buddha was born as Siddhartha into a royal Hindu _____ family.
- **Ⓐ** Brahmin
- **Ⓑ** Kshatriya
- **Ⓒ** Vaishya
- **Ⓓ** Jain

Ans. Ⓑ Kshatriya

Q-15. After how many days of meditation was Buddha said to have attained Enlightenment?
Ans. 49

Q-16. Name the three categories of the Tripitakas.
Ans. Sutras, Abhidharma and Vinaya

Q-17. In which year was the sixth Buddhist council held?
Ans. 1954

Rise of Magadha; the Mauryan Empire Ashoka's inscriptions; his Dharma Nature of the Mauryan state

Q-1. What was the first capital of Magadha?
Ans. Rajagriha

Q-2. Who is the author of the Arthashastra?
Ans. Chanakya/Kautilya

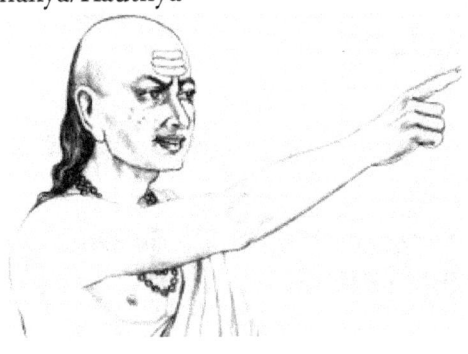

Chanakya

Q-3. Who was the founder of the Mauryan Empire?
Ans. Chandragupta Maurya

Q-4. Towards the end of his life, Chanadragupta Maurya became a _____.
- Ⓐ Buddhist
- Ⓑ Jain
- Ⓒ Muslim
- Ⓓ Hindu

Ans. Ⓑ Jain

Q-5. After which war did Ashoka the Great embrace Buddhism?
Ans. Kalinga war

Q-6. How many spokes does the Ashoka Chakra contain?
Ans. 24

Q-7. What is the national emblem of India?
Ans. Lion capital of Ashoka

Q-8. What was traditionally stored in the *stupas*?
- Ⓐ Money
- Ⓑ Buddhist relics
- Ⓒ Stones
- Ⓓ Jewellery

Ans. Ⓑ Buddhist relics

Q-9. Who wrote a work describing Pataliputra around 300 BCE, titled "Indika"?
Ans. Megasthenes

Q-10. In which year did Ashoka the Great die?
Ans. 232 BCE

Q-11. In which language did Ashoka the Great draft the text of most of his inscriptions?
Ans. Magadhi

Q-12. When the Mauryan empire was divided in half after Ashoka's death, what were the twin capitals?
Ans. Taxila and Pataliputra

Q-13. Who was the last King of the Mauryan Empire who was assassinated by his Senapati Pushyamitra?
Ans. Brihadratha

Q-14. What were the sections in which the Mauryan Cabinet of ministers was divided into?
Ans. Mantrigan and Mantri Parishad

Q-15. Land revenue accounted for _____ of the total Mauryan state revenue.
- Ⓐ One-fifth
- Ⓑ One-tenth
- Ⓒ Half
- Ⓓ One-fourth

Ans. Ⓓ One-fourth

Q-16. Who was the Senapati in the Mauryan government?
Ans. Commander in chief of war

Q-17. The city of Pataliputra was run by a ____ member municipal council.
- Ⓐ 30
- Ⓑ 20
- Ⓒ 10
- Ⓓ 5

Ans. Ⓐ 30

Post-Mauryan Period in Northern and Peninsular India: Political and Administrative History, Society, Economy, Culture and Religion. Tamilaham and its Society: the Sangam Texts

Q-1. Which two dynasties did the Kushans rule in?
Ans. Kadaphises and Kanishkas

Q-2. Which Christian missionary visited India during the rule of Gondophernes?
Ans. Saint Thomas

Q-3. Which two schools of art flourished during the Post-Mauryan period?
Ans. Gandhara and Amravati

Q-4. During the Kushan dynasty, which three ancient Tamil kingdoms involved in internecine warfare began to gain power?
Ans. Chera, Chola and Pandya

Q-5. Who authored "Tolkappiyam", a manual of Tamil grammar?
Ans. Tolkappiyar

Q-6. How many Sangam poems are in existence?
Ans. 2289

Sangam texts

Q-7. Which weapons were illustrated on the royal insignia of the Chera dynasty?
Ans. Bow and arrow

Q-8. In the Sangam age, "Betchi" was the act of taking away which animal by force by the Marwa tribes?
   Ⓐ Horse   Ⓑ Cow
   Ⓒ Goat   Ⓓ Elephant
Ans. Ⓑ Cow

Q-9. Which Sangam port was famous for the export of pearls?
Ans. Korkai

Q-10. Which sage is credited with introducing Vedic religion to the South?
Ans. Sage Agastya

Q-11. Who was the most important God of the Sangam Age?
Ans. Murugan or Subrahmanya

Quiz Time History

Q-12. Where was the first Sangam (assemblage of literary figures) held?
Ans. Madurai

Q-13. The complete Sangam literature is collected in ____ volumes.
- Ⓐ 10
- Ⓑ 6
- Ⓒ 12
- Ⓓ 9

Ans. Ⓓ 9

Q-14. What was the name given to the council of advisors to the King in the Sangam dynasty?
Ans. Pancha Varam

Q-15. Which Chola king committed suicide?
Ans. Kopperuncholan

Q-16. What were the names given to the two main themes of the Sangam poetry?
Ans; Ahm (love and erotica) and Puram (war and valour)

Q-17. Which Chera king won the famous battle of Kongu?
Ans. Kuttuvan

Q-18. Which country did King Ailara conquer and rule over for more than 50 years?
Ans. Sri Lanka

Q-19. In the Sangam Age, what were the taxes paid to the King called?
Ans. Karamai or Pandu

Q-20. Which Roman king did the Pandya rulers send ambassadors to?
Ans. King Augustus

India in the Gupta and post-Gupta Period (to c. 750) : Political History of Northern and Peninsular India; Samanta System and Changes in Political Structure; Economy; Social Structure; Culture; Religion

Q-1. Who founded the Gupta Empire?
Ans. Maharaja Sri-Gupta

Q-2. The Gupta period is called the _____ Age of India.
- Ⓐ Golden
- Ⓑ Silver
- Ⓒ Bronze
- Ⓓ Copper

Ans. Ⓐ Golden

Q-3. Who was the first Chinese pilgrim to visit India during the rule of Chandragupta, the second?
Ans. Fa-Hien

Q-4. Which Gupta Emperor was commonly portrayed as the Indian "Napoleon" by 19th century British historians because of his great military exploits?
Ans. Samudragupta

Q-5. Who forced Ramagupta to sign a peace treaty after the death of Samudragupta?
Ans. The Sakas

Quiz Time History

Q-6. To gain control of the Northern Deccan, to which king did Chandragupta, the second offer his daughter's hand in marriage?
Ans. Rudrasena II

Q-7. In the Gupta era, it was largely the lower class that consumed _____.
- Ⓐ Vegetables
- Ⓑ Meat
- Ⓒ Milk
- Ⓓ Eggs

Ans. Ⓑ Meat

Q-8. Which central Asian invaders did Kumaragupta have to face, who eventually brought the downfall of the Gupta empire?
Ans. The Huns

Q-9. Which of Kalidasa's three plays tells the story of King Dushyant?
Ans. Abhijnanasakuntalam

Q-10. Which religion was revived in the Gupta period?
- Ⓐ Islam
- Ⓑ Jainism
- Ⓒ Buddhism
- Ⓓ Hinduism

Ans. Ⓓ Hinduism

Q-11. When Chandragupta married a daughter of the Licchavi clan, which kingdom did he receive as dowry?
Ans. Magadha

Gold coin depicting Chandragupta

Q-12. Who authored the Kama Sutra?
Ans. Vatsyayana

Q-13. In which place was state-sponsored university founded during the Gupta reign?
Ans. Nalanda

Q-14. In Banabhatta's work, 'Harshacharita', we are told that the Samanta had ___ duties.
   Ⓐ 2   Ⓑ 5
   Ⓒ 6   Ⓓ 8
Ans. Ⓑ 5

Q-15. Name one mathematical contribution of scholars of the Gupta era.
Ans. Quadratic equations or the use of square root of 2 in algebra

Q-16. Where are the most famous Gupta rock-cut temples, famous for statues and frescoes located?
Ans. Ajanta and Ellora

Q-17. Which woman-centric tradition involving suicide, developed fully in the Gupta period?
Ans. Sati

Q-18. Which two sects did the Krishna cult eventually split into?
Ans. Pancharatra and Vaikhanasa

Q-19. Who was the last Gupta to reestablish his authority over Magadha?
Ans. Adityasena

Themes in Early Indian Cultural History: Languages and Texts; Major Stages in the Evolution of Art and Architecture; Major Philosophical Thinkers and Schools; Ideas in Science and Mathematics

Q-1. The Indo-Aryan languages trace their roots to _____.
- Ⓐ Greek
- Ⓑ Latin
- Ⓒ Sanskrit
- Ⓓ Roman

Ans. Ⓒ Sanskrit

Q-2. What does "Arthashastra" mean?

Ans. The science of material gain

Q-3. The Brahmanas are commentaries on the _____.
- Ⓐ Vedas
- Ⓑ Puranas
- Ⓒ Upanishads
- Ⓓ Vedangas

Ans. Ⓐ Vedas

Q-4. What were the two main types of Indian temple traditions?

Ans. Nagara and Dravida

Q-5. In which modern state can the Stone Age Bhimbetka rock paintings be found?

Ans. Madhya Pradesh

Bhimbetka rock paintings

Q-6. Which school of philosophy is Kapila associated with?
Ans. Samkhya

Q-7. Which Indian philosopher authored the popular collection of tales called "The story of the seven wise masters"?
Ans. Syntipas

Q-8. In which 5th century book was the mathematical method of graduated calculation expounded?
Ans. Five principles or Panch Siddhantika

Q-9. What does "Ayurveda" mean?
Ans. Science of life or longevity

Q-10. Around 200 BC, who collected the fundamentals of Yoga and put them together in a treatise called Yogasutra?
Ans. Patanjali

Q-11. Who wrote the oldest Indian medical treatise describing different kinds of surgery called "Sushruta-Samhita"?
Ans. Sushruta

Q-12. Nyaya was a school of Hindu philosophy that studied _____.
- Ⓐ Medicine
- Ⓑ Astronomy
- Ⓒ Logic
- Ⓓ Administration

Ans. Ⓒ Logic

Q-13. How many Purusharthas exist?
Ans. Four

India, 750-1200 : Polity, Society and Economy. Major Dynasties and Political Structures in North India. Agrarian Structures, "Indian Feudalism" and the Rise of Rajputs. The Imperial Cholas and their Contemporaries in Peninsular India. Village Communities in the South, Conditions of Women, Commerce Mercantile Groups and Guilds, Towns, Problem of Coinage, Arab Conquest of Sind; The Ghaznavid Empire

Q-1. What was the armed struggle between the Gurjara Pratiharas, Palas and Rashtrakutas called?
Ans. Tripartite struggle

Q-2. Who was the founder of the Gurjara Pratihara dynasty?
Ans. Nagabhata I

Q-3. What ritual did Dantidurga, the Rashtrakuta leader, perform for the creation of a separate Kshatriya status?
Ans. Hiranyagarbha

Q-4. Which two places did the Palas rule over for almost four decades?
Ans. Bihar and Bengal

Quiz Time History

Q-5. Which king managed to capture Malwa from Nagabhata II?
Ans. Govinda III

Q-6. What was the capital city of the Rashtrakutas?
Ans. Manyakheta or Malkhed

Q-7. Which Sena king was given the title, 'Brahmakshatriya'?
Ans. Samantasena

Q-8. Which dynasty did the Cholas overthrow to come to power in South India?
Ans. Pallavas

Q-9. What title did the Chola king Rajendra I give himself after conquering Bengal?
Ans. Gangaikonda

Q-10. Which king defeated Jodhpur and reestablished the Pratihara rule in Bundelkhand?
Ans. Mihirbhoja

Q-11. Chola King Kulottunga I earned fame by abolishing _____.
- Ⓐ Sati
- Ⓑ Toll tax
- Ⓒ Slavery
- Ⓓ Forced labour

Ans. Ⓑ Toll tax

Q-12. Who were the Samanthas?
- Ⓐ Kings
- Ⓑ Small chiefs
- Ⓒ Servants
- Ⓓ Rajputs

Ans. Ⓑ Small chiefs

Q-13. Which of these was the name given to a non-brahmanical settlement in South India?
- Ⓐ Sabha
- Ⓑ Ur
- Ⓒ Nagada
- Ⓓ Kunda

Ans. Ⓑ Ur

Early and Medieval Indian History

Q-14. Who did the Rajputs oppose when he succeeded the throne of Ghazni?
Ans. Muhammad of Ghor

Q-15. In which place were the Solankis or the Chalukyas based?
Ans. Gujarat

Q-16. Name two new castes that appeared during the post-Gupta period?
Ans. Kayasthas and Khatris

Q-17. Who served as feudal chiefs in most of the Paramara states?
Ans. Thakkuras

Q-18. Which tribal groups received the Rajput rank during this period?
Ans. Medas and Hunas

Q-19. Chola king Rajendra I created an artificial _____ called Gangaikondacholapuram.
    Ⓐ Lake   Ⓑ Dam
    Ⓒ Park   Ⓓ Forest
Ans. Ⓐ Lake

Q-20. Which capital was given the name, "Small Ghazni"?
Ans. Lahore

Q-21. Which family ruled Bengal after the Palas?
Ans. The Senas

Q-22. How many times did the Ghaznavids invade India in retaliation to King Jaypal's invasion?
    Ⓐ 10   Ⓑ 14
    Ⓒ 17   Ⓓ 21
Ans. Ⓒ 17

Q-23. In the post-Gupta period, were land grants taxed?
Ans. No

Q-24. How do we know there was a coin shortage in the post-Gupta period?
Ans. Absence of coins in archeological finds

Coins of the period

Q-25. Which Muslim ruler invaded Sindh by land route in 712 AD?
Ans. Muhammad Bin Kasim

Q-26. Which city did the Arabs call the "City of Gold", due to its great wealth?
Ans. Multan

Q-27. In which battle against Kasim did Sindhi queen Ranibai put up a brave fight?
Ans. The Battle of Raor

Q-28. Who was the first ruler in India to give himself the title of "Sultan"?
Ans. Mahmud Ghaznavi

Q-29. "Jazia" was a tax on _____.
    Ⓐ Non-Muslims   Ⓑ Muslims
    Ⓒ Hindus   Ⓓ Non-Hindus
Ans. Ⓐ Non-Muslims

Q-30. In which year did the Caliph of Persia sentence Kasim to death?
Ans. 716 AD

India, 750-1200: Culture, Literature, Kalhana Historian. Styles of Temple Architecture and Sculpture. Religious Thought and Institutions: Shankaracharya's Vedanta, Ramanuja. Growth of Bhakti, Islam and its Arrival in India. Sufism, Indian Science, Alberuni and his Study of Indian Science and Civilisation

Q-1. The Pala kings were followers of _____.
- Ⓐ Jainism
- Ⓑ Hinduism
- Ⓒ Buddhism
- Ⓓ Islam

Ans. Ⓒ Buddhism

Q-2. Which famous university did Dharampala found near Bhagalpur?
Ans. Vikramashila

Q-3. Which king built the famous Kailasa temple at Ellora?
Ans. Krishna I

Kailasa Temple

Q-4. Who authored the Tamil version of the Ramayana?
Ans. Kamban

Q-5. What was the defining feature of the Nagara temple style?
Ans. Lofty tower called *Shikhara*

Q-6. The Chola rulers were devout worshippers of the _____.
- **A** Kali
- **B** Sun Goddess
- **C** Buddha
- **D** Shiva

Ans. D Shiva

Q-7. Which erotic cult did the elite take an interest in during the Chola period?
Ans. Tantric cult

Q-8. Which famous Vaishnava scholar taught in the temple of Shrirangam for most of his life?
Ans. Ramanuja

Q-9. Who was the author of *Karpuramanjari, Bala Ramayana* and *Kavyamimamsa*?
Ans. Rajasekhara

Q-10. Which of these was not a temple architecture style?
- **A** Nagara
- **B** Dravida
- **C** Vasara
- **D** Ghatika

Ans. D Ghatika

Q-11. What doctrine did Adi Shankara preach?
Ans. Advaita Vedanta

Q-12. How many *mathas* did Adi Shankara create for Hinduism?
- **A** 4
- **B** 6
- **C** 8
- **D** 2

Ans. A 4

Q-13. Under the reign of which King did Kalhana become a court poet?

Ans. Jayasimha

Q-14. Who was Kalhana's teacher?
Ans. Alakadatta

Q-15. How many books is the "Rajatarangini" comprised of?
Ans. 8

Q-16. Who was the most prominent God for Bhakti leader-Ramananda?
Ans. Rama

Q-17. Who is the author of "Bijak" that discusses the existence of a fundamental one?
Ans. Kabir

Q-18. Which saint propagated the "Dvaita" or dual school of philosophy?
Ans. Sri Madhvacharya

Q-19. In which place did the saint Sankaradeva spread the Bhakti teachings?
- Ⓐ Delhi
- Ⓑ Bengal
- Ⓒ Assam
- Ⓓ Tamil Nadu

Ans. Ⓒ Assam

Q-20. Guru Nanak Dev belonged to _____ school.
- Ⓐ Nirguna
- Ⓑ Sarguna
- Ⓒ Doguna
- Ⓓ Saiguna

Ans. Ⓐ Nirguna

Q-21. Which Sufis were the first to compose the Hindavi mystical romances?
Ans. Chishti Sufis

Q-22. Name the two Sufi orders.
Ans. Bashara and Beshara

Quiz Time History

Q-23. Sama and Kawwali are forms of Sufi _____.
 ⓐ Dancing   ⓑ Singing
 ⓒ Writing   ⓓ Mosques
Ans. ⓑ Singing

Q-24. Which group of people first brought Islam to India?
Ans. The Arabs

Q-25. Which group of Indians are said to be the first to convert to Islam?
Ans. Mappilas of Malabar

Q-26. Who built the first Indian mosque in 612 AD?
Ans. Malik Bin Deenar

Q-27. In which battle did the Indian alliance of Gurjaras, Pratiharas and the Chalukyas defeat the Arabs in 738 AD?
Ans. Battle of Rajasthan

Q-28. In which year did Al-Biruni finish his famous book "India"?
Ans. 1030 AD

Q-29. What was Al-Biruni's major work on astronomy?
Ans. Qanun al-Mas'udi

Q-30. Al-Biruni is often referred to as the Father of _____.
 ⓐ Astronomy   ⓑ Medicine
 ⓒ Religion   ⓓ Geodesy
Ans. ⓓ Geodesy

The 13th Century: The Ghorian Invasions, Factors Behind Ghorian Success, Economic, Social and Cultural Consequences. Foundation of the Delhi Sultanate. The "Slave" Dynasty: IItutmish, Balban. The Khilji Revolution and the Early Sultanate Architecture

Q-1. Which empire reached its peak under the brothers, Shamsuddin Muhammad and Shihabuddin (Muizzuddin)?
Ans. The Ghurid Empire

Q-2. In which year did Muizzuddin capture Multan?
Ans. 1175 AD

Q-3. Which region did the Gahadavala King, Jayachandra rule over?
Ans. Kannauj

Q-4. Which three regions did Qutubuddin Aibak and the Turks conquer?
Ans. Kalinjar, Mohaba and Khajuraho

Q-5. Who captured Bihar and Bengal during this period?
Ans. Bakhtiyar Khilji

Q-6. A member of the ____ tribe assassinated Muizzuddin Muhammad on the banks of the river, Jhelum.
- Ⓐ Kohar
- Ⓑ Kokkhar
- Ⓒ Lopiya
- Ⓓ Laddiya

Ans. Ⓑ Kokkhar

Quiz Time History

Q-7. Who was Muizzuddin Muhammad's most important slave and subsequent ruler of Ghazni?
Ans. Tajuddin Yilduz

Q-8. Iltutmish was Qutubuddin Aibak's _____.
- Ⓐ Son
- Ⓑ Grandson
- Ⓒ Slave
- Ⓓ Son-in-law

Ans. Ⓓ Son-in-law

Q-9. In which year was Iltutmish consecrated as the Sultan of Delhi?
Ans. 1129 AD

Q-10. Which famous group of forty slaves was Balban the most powerful member of?
Ans. Group of Forty or Chalisa

Q-11. The Mamluk dynasty is another name of the ____ dynasty.
- Ⓐ Bengal
- Ⓑ Slave
- Ⓒ Rajput
- Ⓓ Punjab

Ans. Ⓑ Slave

Q-12. Who was the last Khwarazm ruler?
Ans. Jalaluddin

Q-13. Which ancient temple did Iltutmish destroy after he conquered Ujjain?
Ans. Mahakal temple

Q-14. "Dagh" involved the branding of which animal?
- Ⓐ Cow
- Ⓑ Ox
- Ⓒ Horse
- Ⓓ Camel

Ans. Ⓒ Horse

Q-15. In which year did Changez Khan reach the Indus?
Ans. 1221 AD

Q-16. Aram Baksh was the son of _____.
- Ⓐ Iltutmish
- Ⓑ Muizzuddin Muhammad
- Ⓒ Qutubuddin Aibak
- Ⓓ Jalaluddin

Ans. Ⓒ Qutubuddin Aibak

Q-17. How many ruling dynasties did the Sultanate of Delhi have?
Ans. 5

Q-18. Who was the first female ruler of medieval India?
Ans. Razia Sultan

Q-19. Which famous Sufi saint is the Qutub Minar named after?
Ans. Khwaja Qutubuddin Bakhtiar Kaki

Qutub Minar

Q-20. Which Khilji Sultan was murdered by Khusrau Khan?
Ans. Mubarak Shah

Quiz Time History

Q-21. What does the word, "Mamluk" mean?
Ans. Slave born of free parents

Q-22. Jalaluddin ascended the throne at the age of ____.
   Ⓐ 18   Ⓑ 60
   Ⓒ 80   Ⓓ 70
Ans. Ⓓ 70

Q-23. Which two departments did Balban separate when he came to power?
   Ⓐ Trade and Finance   Ⓑ Finance and Military affairs
   Ⓒ Trade and Military affairs Ⓓ Military affairs and Tax affairs
Ans. Ⓑ Finance and Military affairs

Q-24. Which to-be-Sultan invaded Devagiri during Jalaluddin's reign?
Ans. Ali Gurshap (later Sultan Alauddin Khilji)

Q-25. Who married Razia Sultan after defeating her in battle?
Ans. Altunia

Q-26. The Quwwat-ul-islam mosque in Delhi was originally a ____ temple.
   Ⓐ Jain   Ⓑ Kali
   Ⓒ Rama   Ⓓ Shiva
Ans. Ⓐ Jain

Q-27. The Arch and ____ method was an important Sultanate architectural style.
   Ⓐ Tower   Ⓑ Dome
   Ⓒ Beam   Ⓓ Slab
Ans. Ⓑ Dome

Q-28. Which script was often used in the Sultanate architecture?
Ans. Arabic

Early and Medieval Indian History

Q-29. Which of these was not used by the Turks in their architectural representations?
- Ⓐ Flowers
- Ⓑ Coloured stones
- Ⓒ Human and animal figures
- Ⓓ Script

Ans. Ⓒ Human and animal figures

Q-30. How tall is the Qutub Minar?
Ans. About 72.5 metres

The 14th Century: Alauddin Khilji's Conquests, Agrarian and Economic Measures. Muhammad bin Tughluq's Major Projects. Firuz Tughluq's Concessions and Public Works and Decline of the Sultanate. Foreign Contacts: Ibn Battuta

Q-1. Alauddin claimed a majority of war booty, and left only _____ to the soldiers.
- **Ⓐ** One-tenth
- **Ⓑ** Half
- **Ⓒ** One-third
- **Ⓓ** One-fifth

Ans. **Ⓓ** One-fifth

Q-2. Which new economic body was created by Alauddin to collect taxes and arrears from citizens?

Ans. Diwan-i-Mustakhraj

Q-3. Which region did Alauddin capture from Hamir Deva, descendant of Prithviraj III?

Ans. Ranthambhor

Q-4. Who invaded the Sultanate six times during the first four years of Alauddin's reign?

Ans. The Mongols

Q-5. "Shuna" was the name given to a controller of a _____.
- **Ⓐ** Market
- **Ⓑ** Village
- **Ⓒ** Granary
- **Ⓓ** Tax office

Ans. **Ⓐ** Market

Q-6. Who was the king of Gujarat when Alauddin conquered it?
Ans. King Karna

Q-7. Which place did Alauddin rename Khizrabad after his son Khizr Khan?
Ans. Chittor

Q-8. The regulation of _____ was related to the measurement of cultivable land, to decide land revenue.
    Ⓐ Biswa   Ⓑ Zabita
    Ⓒ Shuhna   Ⓓ Ragut
Ans. Ⓑ Zabita

Q-9. Initially, the word, "Tughluq" was not the name of a tribe or clan, but the personal name of a Sultan. Name him.
Ans. Ghiyasuddin

Q-10. Which Tughluq ruler was also called Jauna Khan and Illugh Khan?
Ans. Muhammad bin Tughluq

Q-11. Due to a shortage of silver, Muhammad bin Tughluq introduced a token currency system, where _____ replaced silver.
    Ⓐ Lead   Ⓑ Gold
    Ⓒ Brass   Ⓓ Bronze
Ans. Ⓓ Bronze

Sultanate coins

Quiz Time History

Q-12. Where did Muhammad bin Tughluq lead his army after his conquest of Qarachil, which resulted in their complete annihilation?
Ans. Tibet

Q-13. Towards the end of his reign, in which region did Muhammad bin Tughluq increase the land revenue when it was in the middle of famine and plague?
Ans. Doab

Q-14. Kharaj, Zakat, Jeziah and Khams were types of ____.
- **Ⓐ** Laws
- **Ⓑ** Taxes
- **Ⓒ** Coins
- **Ⓓ** Markets

Ans. **Ⓑ** Taxes

Q-15. What was the name of the body, Firoz Shah Tughluq created to look after the needs of the impoverished?
Ans. Diwan-i-khairat

Q-16. Which tax did Firoz Shah levy on Brahmins to show his religious leanings?
Ans. Jeziah

Q-17. Which famous temple in Puri did Firoz Shah destroy?
Ans. Jagannath Temple

Q-18. Firoz Shah ruled as a deputy of ____'s son.
- **Ⓐ** Timur
- **Ⓑ** Qutubuddin
- **Ⓒ** Mubarak Shah
- **Ⓓ** Shahrukh

Ans. **Ⓐ** Timur

Q-19. Which two new types of coins did Firoz Shah issue?
Ans. Tankk and Jital

Early and Medieval Indian History

Q-20. In which year did Firoz Shah die?
Ans. 1388 AD

Q-21. Who was the founder of the Sayyid dynasty?
Ans. Khizr Khan

Q-22. Which conquest in 1484 AD was Bahlul Lodi's greatest political feat?
Ams: Sharqi kingdom of Jaunpur

Q-23. Who shifted the capital to Agravan (Agra) to tackle the Rajputs?
Ans. Sikandar Shah

Q-24. What was the birthplace of Ibn Battuta?
Ans. Tangiers, Morocco

Q-25. Which work of Ibn Battuta gives a description of Constantinople and Saray?
Ans. Rihlah or Book of Travels

Q-26. Which Sultan appointed Ibn Battuta as the chief justice of Delhi?
Ans. Muhammad bin Tughluq

Q-27. In 1342, Ibn Battuta was appointed the ambassador to _____.
- Ⓐ Japan
- Ⓑ China
- Ⓒ Tibet
- Ⓓ Sri Lanka

Ans. Ⓑ China

Q-28. When Ibn Battuta moved to Fez, who asked him to record his writings for posterity?
Ans. Sultan Abu Inan

Q-29. Who was the Emperor of Constantinople in 1332 when Ibn Battuta visited it?
Ans. Andronicus III

Q-30. Who was the scholar who assisted Ibn Battuta in recording and writing "Rihlah"?
Ans. Ibn Juzayy

Economy, Society and Culture in the 13th and 14th centuries. Caste and Slavery under the Sultanate. Technological Changes. Sultanate Architecture, [Persian Literature: Amir Khusrau, Historiography; Ziya Barani. Evolution of a Composite Culture. Sufism in North India, Lingayats and Bhakti Schools in the South

Q-1. Which famous traveller made it clear in his works that Sati was strictly optional?
Ans. Ibn Battuta

Q-2. Which ruler constructed a network of canals from the Sutlej, Ghaggar and Kali rivers?
Ans. Firoz Shah Tughluq

Q-3. Which new metallurgy technique emerged during this period that allowed people to use cheap copper vessels for cooking?
Ans. Tin-coating

Q-4. What was the name of a famous monastery in Ajmer which was converted into a mosque when the Turks first came to India?
Ans. Arhai din ka Jhonpra

Quiz Time History

Q-5. What was the name of the door added to the Qutub Minar by Alauddin?
Ans. Alai Darwaza

Q-6. The Kotla fort in Delhi was built by _____.
    Ⓐ Alauddin   Ⓑ Firoz Shah Tughluq
    Ⓒ Balban   Ⓓ Muhammad bin Tughluq
Ans. Ⓑ Firoz Shah Tughluq

Q-7. Sericulture increased the production of _____, which made India import less of it from Iran and Afghanistan.
    Ⓐ Cotton   Ⓑ Precious stones
    Ⓒ Silk   Ⓓ Rice
Ans. Ⓒ Silk

Q-8. Who has been called the "Prince of Moneyers"?
Ans. Muhammad bin Tughluq

Q-9. Even though sloping walls and use of batter are features of Tughluq architecture, in which ruler's buildings do we find these missing?
Ans. Firoz Shah Tughluq

Q-10. What is the shape of most of the tombs in the Lodhi Garden?
Ans. Octagonal

Lodhi Garden

Q-11. "Zimmis" were another name given to _____.
- Ⓐ Muslims
- Ⓑ Non-Muslims
- Ⓒ Sultans
- Ⓓ Slaves

Ans. Ⓑ Non-Muslims

Q-12. What were loyal slaves well-trained in battle called?
Ans. Mamluks

Q-13. What were the state laws that the Sultans imposed themselves to practically solve disputes among people?
- Ⓐ Shariah
- Ⓑ Ulema
- Ⓒ Zawabit
- Ⓓ Jeziyah

Ans. Ⓒ Zawabit

Q-14. In which year was Amir Khusrau born?
Ans. 1252 AD

Q-15. Name the new style of Persian language created by Amir Khusrau.
Ans. Sabaq-i-Hind

Q-16. Who was the Sufi saint who was famous for his religious, musical samas or gatherings?
Ans. Nizamuddin Auliya

Q-17. What was Ziauddin Barani's most famous work?
Ans. Tarikh-i-Firuz Shahi

Q-18. Fatawa-i-Jahandari is a book of instructions on _____.
- Ⓐ Music
- Ⓑ Treatment of slaves
- Ⓒ Trade
- Ⓓ State affairs

Ans. Ⓓ State affairs

Q-19. What was the basic doctrine of the Sufis?
Ans. Wahadat-ul-wujud or "Unity of the Being"

Quiz Time History

Q-20. Who was the founder of the Chishti Sufi order?
Ans. Sheikh Moinuddin Chishti

Q-21. Which Sufi order did Bahauddin Zakariya belong to?
Ans. Suhrawardi order

Q-22. The main exponent of the Lingayats, Basava was originally a ____.
  Ⓐ Jain   Ⓑ Hindu
  Ⓒ Muslim   Ⓓ Buddhist
Ans. Ⓐ Jain

Q-23. In which place did the Lingayat sect first develop?
Ans. Karnataka

Q-24. Name the first Sultan who freed himself from the strict influence of the Ulemas?
Ans. Alauddin Khilji

Q-25. In south India, which two groups of saints showed a renewed interest in Vaishnava and Shiva worship?
Ans. Alvar and Nayanmar (Nayanar)

Q-26. Which famous female poet was known for the erotic element in the southern Bhakti poetry?
Ans. Andal or Kodai

Q-27. Which two Bhakti saints have been described as "untouchables"?
Ans. Nandanar and Tiruppan Alvar

Q-28. Who among these is not one of the legendary Lingayat teachers?
  Ⓐ Renuka   Ⓑ Daruka
  Ⓒ Uma   Ⓓ Vishvakarna
Ans. Ⓒ Uma

Q-29. What is the name of the "linga" that is worn by both male and females members of the Lingayat sect?

Ans. Ishtalinga

Q-30. "Shivajnanabodham" by Meykanda contains the basic doctrine of which school of Shaivism?

Ans. Shaiva Siddhanta

The 15th and early 16th Century (Political History). Rise of Provincial Dynasties: Bengal, Kashmir (Zainul Abedin), Gujarat, Malwa and Bahmanids. The Vijayanagara Empire, the Lodis, the Mughal Empire, First Phase : Babur and Humayun. The Sur Empire : Sher Shah's Administration. The Portuguese Colonial Enterprise

Q-1. In which year was the Vijayanagara empire founded?
Ans 1336 AD

Q-2. Under which Kakatiya ruler's service were the Sangama brothers before they founded their empire?
Ans. Prataparudra II

Q-3. With which Sultans did the Vijayanagara rulers battle with for nearly four decades before defeating them in 1377 AD?
Ans. Sultans of Madurai

Q-4. The attack on which fortress in the Tungabhadra doab started the Vijayanagar-Bahmani conflict?
Ans. Fortress of Mudkal

Q-5. Under Harihara II, the Vijayanagara empire looked to expand towards the _____ sea coast.
- **Ⓐ** Western
- **Ⓑ** Eastern
- **Ⓒ** Southern
- **Ⓓ** Northern

Ans. Ⓑ Eastern

Early and Medieval Indian History

Q-6. Which Sangama ruler strengthened his army by making the Muslim recruits teach the Hindus the art of archery?
Ans. Deva Raya II

Q-7. Which ruler was executed after the battle of Raksasa Tangadi in 1565 AD?
Ans. Rama Raja

Q-8. Which Portuguese governor offered help to Krishnadeva in his battle against the Bahmanis?
Ans. Albuquerque

Q-9. When Krishnadeva defeated Prataparudra, which territory did he gain complete control over?
Ans. Telangana

Q-10. Who was the founder of the Barid Shahis of Bidar?
Ans. Ali Barid

Q-11. Which Brahmin zamindar of Dinajpur seized the throne of Bengal in 1415 AD?
Ans. Raja Ganesh

Q-12. Ruknuddin Barbak Shah had the military help of the_____ slaves while defeating the Hindu rulers of Orissa and Kamarupa?
- Ⓐ Ethiopian
- Ⓑ Egyptian
- Ⓒ Tanzanian
- Ⓓ Nigerian

Ans. Ⓐ Ethiopian

Q-13. Which ruler of Bengal defeated the Abyssinians?
Ans. Alauddin Hussain Shah

Q-14. In which year did Sher Shah capture Gaur?
Ans. 1538 AD

Q-15. Who was known as the "Aurangzeb of Kashmir"?
Ans. Sikandar

Q-16. Which benevolent Muslim ruler corrected many wrongs of his successor, Sikandar, including repairing destroyed temples and improved administration?
Ans. Zainul Abidin

Q-17. Name the most powerful ruler of Malwa who ruled between 1436 and 1439 AD.
Ans. Mahmud Khilji I

Q-18. Babur was the _____ of Timur Lenk.
    Ⓐ Son   Ⓑ Grandson
    Ⓒ Great grandson   Ⓓ Father
Ans. Ⓒ Great grandson

Q-19. In which famous battle did Babur defeat Ibrahim Lodhi?
Ans. The First Battle of Panipat

Q-20. After winning the battle of Khanwa, which place did Babur occupy?
Ans. Agra

Q-21. Babur left behind his autobiography called _____.
    Ⓐ Babur Namah   Ⓑ Babri-Khitaab
    Ⓒ Babri Dastaak   Ⓓ Tuzuk-i-Babri
Ans. Ⓓ Tuzuk-i-Babri

Early and Medieval Indian History

Q-22. In which year did Humayun first ascend the throne?
Ans. 1536 AD

Q-23. After losing at the hands of Sher Shah, where did Humayun flee to and spend 10 years?
Ans. Persia

Q-24. In which battle did Humayun defeat Sikandar Sur?
Ans. Battle of Sirhind

Q-25. For how many years did Sher Shah Suri rule?
  Ⓐ 6   Ⓑ 5
  Ⓒ 10   Ⓓ 8
Ans. Ⓑ 5

Q-26. In which year did Humayun reconquer India by defeating the Afghans?
Ans. 1555 AD

Q-27. Near which southwestern port did Vasco da Gama's fleet arrive in 1498 AD?
Ans. Calicut

Q-28. The Portuguese were essentially interested in gaining control of the _____ trade.
  Ⓐ Spice   Ⓑ Cloth
  Ⓒ Rice   Ⓓ Horse
Ans. Ⓐ Spice

Q-29. Which Sultan gave Sher Shah Suri the title, "Sher Khan"?
Ans. Sultan Muhammad Nuhani

Q-30. In which famous battle in 1536 AD did Sher Shah destroy almost all the Mughal forces and cause Humayun to flee across the Ganges?
Ans. Battle of Chausa

The 15th and Early 16th Century (Society, Economy and Culture). Regional Cultures and Literatures, Provincial Architectural Styles. Society, Culture, Literature and the Arts in Vijayanagara Empire. Monotheistic Movements: Kabir and Guru Nanak. Bhakti Movements: Chaitanya, Sufism in its Pantheistic Phase

Q-1. Which work by Sri Krishnadevaraya provides a good idea about the political ideas of the Vijayanagar rulers?
Ans. Amuktamalyada

Q-2. What was the name given to gold coins issued by the Vijayanagara emperors?
Ans. Varahas

Q-3. Some coins contained the image of a Gandaberunda, which was a _____.
- **Ⓐ** Lion
- **Ⓑ** Bull
- **Ⓒ** Eagle
- **Ⓓ** Tiger

Ans. Ⓒ Eagle

Q-4. Which king was a patron of the arts and was fondly called 'Andhra Bhoja'?
Ans. Krishnadevaraya

Q-5. What was the name given to the special group of eight writers and poets of literature in the court of 'Andhra Bhoja'?
Ans. Ashtadiggajas

Q-6. Which city did Krishnadevaraya build in memory of his mother, Nagamba?
Ans. Nagalapura

Q-7. "Gauda" was the name given to the village _____.
- **A** Feudal chief
- **B** Tax collector
- **C** Moneylender
- **D** Headman

Ans. **D** Headman

Q-8. Who built the Grand Trunk Road (GT Road) that connects Peshawar to Calcutta?
Ans. Sher Shah Suri

Q-9. Who was the painter Humayun met at Tabriz, who later tutored Akbar?
Ans. Abdus Samad

Q-10. In what style was the manuscript Dastan-e-Amir Hamza illustrated?
Ans. Safavid Style

Q-11. The "pietra dura" style invloves decorating walls or ceilings with carved _____ designs and semi-precious stones.
- **A** Animal
- **B** Floral
- **C** Abstract
- **D** Textual

Ans. **B** Floral

Q-12. Which crop was most widely exported from Vijayanagara?
Ans. Black pepper

Q-13. How many schools did the teachings of Ramananda create?
Ans. Two

Q-14. Which bhakti school did Chaitanya, Mirabai and Tulsidas belong to?
Ans. Saguna

Mirabai

Q-15. Which famous ruler supposedly persecuted Kabir?
Ans. Sikandar Lodi

Q-16. The Nirguna school believed in a God with ____ form/s.
    Ⓐ no   Ⓑ mutliple
    Ⓒ two   Ⓓ three
Ans. Ⓐ no

Q-17. What was the birthplace of Guru Nanak?
Ans. Talwandi

Q-18. Which Guru started the Gurmukhi script?
Ans. Guru Angad

Q-19. "Langar" was created to abolish the ____ system.
    Ⓐ religious   Ⓑ caste
    Ⓒ slave   Ⓓ trade
Ans. Ⓑ caste

Early and Medieval Indian History

Q-20. In which year was the Adi Granth compiled?
Ans. 1604 AD

Q-21. Who authored Ramcharitmanas?
Ans. Tulsidas

Q-22. Which Bhakti saint travelled extensively and had discussions with Sufi saints in Delhi?
Ans. Namadeva

Q-23. What does the Sufi concept "tark-e-duniya" mean?
Ans. Renunciation of the world

Q-24. _____ was the foreign traveller who visited the Vijayanagara kingdom in the time of Achyuta Deva Raya.
- **A** Alonzo Queba
- **B** Sebastian Morle
- **C** Fernao Nuniz
- **D** Domingo Paes

Ans. **C** Fernao Nuniz

Q-25. Which Sufi saint was called 'Siddha' or perfect?
Ans. Nizamuddin Auliya

Q-26. Where was Kabir's tomb built?
Ans. Magahar

Q-27. What was "asthavana"?
Ans. Land revenue department

Q-28. The Sahaja cult influenced the literature of which language?
- **A** Hindi
- **B** Oriya
- **C** Bengali
- **D** Tamil

Ans. **C** Bengali

Q-29. Bhakti Kala was the ____ stage of hindi literature.
- Ⓐ Second
- Ⓑ First
- Ⓒ Third
- Ⓓ Last

Ans. Ⓐ Second

Q-30. Which Guru wrote Sukhmani?

Ans. Guru Arjan Dev

Akbar: His Conquests and Consolidation of Empire. Establishment of Jagir and Mansab Systems and His Rajput Policy. Evolution of Religious and Social Outlook. Theory of Sulh-i-kul and Religious Policy. Abul Fazl, Thinker and Historian, Court Patronage of Art and Technology

Q-1. At what age did Akbar ascend the throne?
Ans. 13 years

Q-2. Who was appointed as Akbar's regent in 1556 AD?
Ans. Bairam Khan

Q-3. Which kingdom ruled by Rana Uday Singh put up a brave fight when Akbar attacked it?
Ans. Mewar

Q-4. Which Rajput ruler's daughter did Akbar marry to display his goodwill towards the Hindus?
Ans. Raja Todar Mal

Q-5. Where was Akbar's capital moved to in 1585 AD?
Ans. Lahore

Q-6. What name did Akbar give to new religion he created?
Ans. Din-e-Ilahi

Q-7. What system did Akbar introduce to organise the nobility and army?
Ans. The Mansabdari System

Quiz Time History

Q-8. Which Sufi saint was Akbar's most favourite religious advisor?
Ans. Sheik Salim Chishti

Q-9. In which year was Fatehpur Sikri completed?
Ans. 1578 AD

Q-10. In 1568 AD, which fort was seized, leading to the complete control of Mewar by the Mughals?
Ans. The Chittorgarh Fort

Q-11. In which year did Akbar invade Gujarat?
Ans. 1572 AD

Q-12. Who authored the book, Ain-i-Akbari that discusses the rules of Abkar's reign?
Ans. Abul Fazl

Q-13. Akbar's _____ Muhammad Hakim was the ruler of Kabul who battled with Akbar in Lahore.
- Ⓐ Son
- Ⓑ Cousin
- Ⓒ Brother
- Ⓓ Half-brother

Ans. Ⓓ Half-brother

Q-14. Which of these four Sultans of the South agreed to submit to Akbar's rule?
- Ⓐ Khandesh
- Ⓑ Bijapur
- Ⓒ Golconda
- Ⓓ Ahmadnagar

Ans. Ⓐ Khandesh

Q-15. Sulh-e-Kul was the concept of universal _____.
- Ⓐ Trade
- Ⓑ Harmony
- Ⓒ Praise
- Ⓓ Rule

Ans. Ⓑ Harmony

Q-16. Akbar divided his empire into _____ provinces called "subahs".
- Ⓐ 12
- Ⓑ 14
- Ⓒ 21
- Ⓓ 22

Ans. Ⓒ 21

Q-17. What was the name given to the head of sea ports?
Ans. Shah Bandars

Q-18. Which Rajput king did Akbar work with to issue a revenue schedule that would help both peasants and the state?
Ans. Todar Mal

Q-19. Khudkasta was a certain class of _____.
- Ⓐ Zamindar
- Ⓑ Trader
- Ⓒ Peasant
- Ⓓ Ruler

Ans. Ⓒ Peasant

Q-20. What was Akbar's most important system for fixing land revenue?
Ans. Karori System

Q-21. Which group of priests did Akbar welcome in his court in 1580 AD, who gave him a copy of the Polyglot Bible?
Ans. Jesuit priests

Q-22. Who started building Akbar's tomb near Sikandra?
- Ⓐ Akbar himself
- Ⓑ Jahangir
- Ⓒ Todar Mal
- Ⓓ Khan Fazal

Ans. Ⓐ Akbar himself

Akbar's tomb

Q-23. What was "chehra" ot "toshiba"?
Ans. Descriptive roll of soldiers

Q-24. What were the dual ranks of the Mansabdari system?
Ans. Zat and Sawar

Q-25. From 1575 AD onwards, what was used instead of rope for measuring land?
Ans. Tanab: Bamboo sticks joined by iron rings

Q-26. As the Muslims had to abide by the Sharia, what law did the Hindus abide by?
Ans. Dharmashastra

Q-27. Which Kashmiri prince fought valiantly against Akbar, even after his father Ali Shah surrendered?
Ans. Yaqub

Q-28. In which year was the Battle of Haldighati fought?
Ans. 1576 AD

Q-29. Whom did Akbar appoint as his prime minister in 1561 AD?
Ans. Shamsuddin Muhammad Atgah Khan

Q-30. What significant religious space was created at Fatehpur Sikri in 1575 AD to bring saints and mystics from all religions together?
Ans. Ibadat Khana or House of Worship

Mughal Empire in the 17th Century: Major Policies (Administrative and Religious) of Jahangir, Shah Jahan and Aurangzeb, The Empire and the Zamindars. Nature of the Mughal State. Late 17th Century Crisis: Revolts, The Ahom Kingdom, Shivaji and the Early Maratha Kingdom

Q-1. In which year did Jahangir ascend the Mughal throne?
Ans. 1605 AD

Q-2. Which two rulers assisted Khusrau when he revolted against the king?
Ans. Hussain Baig of Agra and Diwan Abdul Rahim of Lahore

Q-3. Which Sikh Guru did Jahangir execute in 1606 AD?
Ans. Guru Arjan Dev

Q-4. Jahangir's famous wife Nur Jahan belonged to _____.
  Ⓐ Lahore   Ⓑ Kabul
  Ⓒ Persia   Ⓓ Afghanistan
Ans. Ⓒ Persia

Q-5. Which two independent kingdoms in the South strongly resisted Jahangir's invasions?
Ans. Ahmadnagar and Asirgarh

Q-6. Jahangir gave _____ the title of Shah Jahan.
  Ⓐ Khusrau Ⓑ Pervez
  Ⓒ Shahriyar Ⓓ Khurram
Ans. Ⓓ Khurram

Q-7. Who arrested Jahangir and Nur Jahan, after revolting in 1626 AD?
Ans. Mahabat Khan

Q-8. Which representative of the East India Company visited Jahangir in 1608 AD?
Ans. Captain William Hawkins

Q-9. In which year did Jahangir capture the fort of Kangra?
Ans. 1620 AD

Q-10. Shah Jahan used his administrative skills to reduce damage in _____ that was affected by famine in 1630-1632 AD.
  Ⓐ Gujarat Ⓑ Lucknow
  Ⓒ Lahore Ⓓ Malwa
Ans. Ⓐ Gujarat

Q-11. Name the Governor of Bengal in 1632 AD, who was given the task to stop the Portuguese missionaries from spreading Christianity.
Ans. Kasim Khan

Q-12. Which dynasty did Shah Jahan bring under the Mughal rule in 1633 AD?
Ans. Nizam Shahi's dynasty of Ahmadnagar

Q-13. In which year did Shah Jahan reconquer Kandahar (Afghanistan)?
Ans. 1638 AD

Early and Medieval Indian History

Q-14. After defeating the rulers of Bijapur and Golkonda, whom did Shah Jahan appoint as Governor in charge of the Deccan affairs?

Ans. Aurangzeb

Q-15. What title did Aurangzeb assume after he was crowned the ruler?

Ans. Alamgir

Q-16. Who's execution in 1689 AD caused the collapse of the Maratha Empire?

Ans. Sambhaji

Q-17. In which year did the Persian and Afghan armies invade Delhi, taking with them the famous Peacock throne?

Ans. 1739 AD

Peacock Throne

Q-18. Which group of people were significant in controlling the land revenue system?

Ans. Zamindars

Q-19. Which of these was not a class of peasants?
- Ⓐ Khudkasta
- Ⓑ Pahis
- Ⓒ Keetiyars
- Ⓓ Muzaruyams

Ans. Ⓒ Keetiyars

Quiz Time History

Q-20. The Batai or Galla-bakhi was a _____ portion of produce under the system that officials claimed.
- Ⓐ Rightful
- Ⓑ Wrong
- Ⓒ Small
- Ⓓ Large

Ans. Ⓐ Rightful

Q-21. What does the title "Chhatrapati" mean?
Ans. Lord of the Universe

Q-22. In which year did the Mughals and Marathas sign a treaty, allowing the Marathas to rule the Deccan, while acknowledging the Mughal sovereignty in theory?
Ans. 1717 AD

Q-23. Rajaram was Sambhaji's _____.
- Ⓐ Son
- Ⓑ Brother
- Ⓒ Father
- Ⓓ Uncle

Ans. Ⓑ Brother

Q-24. Which place did Ali Adil Shah rule over?
Ans. Bijapur

Q-25. After which incident in 1664 AD, did Aurangzeb realise Shivaji was a significant force?
Ans. Sacking of Surat

Q-26. Which 17th century chronicler recorded the warfare style of the Ahoms?
Ans. Abdul Hamid Lahori

Q-27. The Ahom society was divided into clans or _____.
- Ⓐ Khels
- Ⓑ Bhels
- Ⓒ Pittiyas
- Ⓓ Korubas

Ans. Ⓐ Khels

Q-28. What was the name given to the historical works first written in Ahom, and later in Assamese?
Ans. Buranjis

Early and Medieval Indian History

Q-29. Which Ahom ruler built Rangpur and established trade with Tibet?
Ans. Rudra Singha

Q-30. What long Ahom civil war or uprising contributed to their downfall?
Ans. Moamaria uprising

Economy and Society, 16th and 17th Centuries: Population, Agricultural and Craft Production. Towns, Commerce with Europe through Dutch, English and French Companies- A Trade Revolution. Indian Mercantile Classes: Banking, Insurance and Credit Systems. Conditions of Peasants, Famines, Condition of Women

Q-1. Which of these metals played a significant role in the 16th and 17th century artillery creation by the Portuguese?
- **Ⓐ** Steel
- **Ⓑ** Brass
- **Ⓒ** Bronze
- **Ⓓ** Iron

Ans. **Ⓓ** Iron

Q-2. Who was the first ruler who introduced the use of heavy cannons in the imperial army?
Ans. Islam Shah

Q-3. In which years did plague continuously cause death and destruction throughout central and northern India?
- **Ⓐ** 1595-98 AD
- **Ⓑ** 1545-48 AD
- **Ⓒ** 1603-05 AD
- **Ⓓ** 1648-51 AD

Ans. **Ⓐ** 1595-98 AD

Early and Medieval Indian History

Q-4. In 1769-70 AD, famines killed over one-third of the population in ____.
- **A** Punjab
- **B** Delhi
- **C** Lahore
- **D** Bengal

Ans. D Bengal

Q-5. Trade connections opened by the Portuguese, French, Dutch and English stimulated the production of what kind of textiles in India?

Ans. Cotton

Q-6. In which year did the French arrive in India?

Ans. 1664 AD

Q-7. Where did the Dutch traders set up their first factory in India?

Ans. Masulipatnam

Q-8. After which Englishman's visit in 1619 AD, were they allowed to establish a factory in Surat?

Ans. Sir Thomas Roe

Q-9. Sher Shah Suri changed the currency to finely minted ____ coins called "dam".
- **A** Silver
- **B** Brass
- **C** Bronze
- **D** Gold

Ans. A Silver

Q-10. Purdah was largely a practice for the ____ class.
- **A** Middle
- **B** Lower
- **C** Upper
- **D** Lower-middle

Ans. C Upper

Q-11. Name three new crops the farmers started cultivating during this period.

Ans. Tobacco, Maize, Potato, Chilly (Any three)

Quiz Time History

Q-12. Agra, Patna, Khambayat and Paithan were famous for _____ cloth.
- Ⓐ Cotton
- Ⓑ Silk
- Ⓒ Crepe
- Ⓓ Khadi

Ans. Ⓑ Silk

Q-13. What was the name given to the gold coins minted by the Mughals?

Ans. Mohurs

Gold coins/mohurs

Q-14. Name two items that India was famous for exporting.

Ans. Spices, textiles, medicinal herbs and indigo (Any two)

Q-15. The words "baqqal" and "banyan" were often used interchangeably. What did they mean?
- Ⓐ King and subject
- Ⓑ Slave and ruler
- Ⓒ Grain merchant and Traditional merchant
- Ⓓ Man and wife

Ans. Ⓒ Grain merchant and Traditional merchant

Q-16. Which was the most important port with regard to the Indian merchant capital in the Mughal period?

Ans. Cambay port, Surat

Q-17. What was the name given to local moneylenders who acted as deposit bankers?

Ans. Sarrafs

Q-18. Which two towns in Punjab became production centres for dagger, knives and ornamental swords?

Ans. Wazirabad and Nizamabad

Early and Medieval Indian History

Q-19. Name the type of slipper first created in Sind with a colourful pompom on top that resembled its Greek counterpart.
Ans. Triguli

Q-20. What was the main product of trade between Coromandel and Malacca?
Ans. Cloth

Q-21. In which year did Van Khesteyan sign a treaty with Khurram?
Ans. 1618 AD

Q-22. Which Queen signed the charter to create the English East India Company?
Ans. Queen Elizabeth I

Q-23. Which ruler granted the English a "farman" in 1691 AD, exempting the Company from paying custom duties in Bengal?
Ans. Aurangzeb

Q-24. Which French governor tried to regroup the French power in India and threatened the British supremacy?
Ans. Dupleix

Q-25. What loan did the Mughal administration introduce to encourage agricultural production?
Ans. Takkawi

Q-26. In the Mughal era, by what age were most girls betrothed?
Ans. 10 years

Q-27. Sarai were ___ along the roads and highways.
- Ⓐ Hospitals
- Ⓑ Inns
- Ⓒ Bath houses
- Ⓓ Stables

Ans. Ⓑ Inns

Quiz Time History

Q-28. Which Mughal ruler patronised the carpet making industry?
Ans. Akbar

Q-29. Around 1700 AD, the approximate population of the Mughal Empire was ____.
    Ⓐ 50-60 million   Ⓑ 80-90 million
    Ⓒ 110-130 million   Ⓓ 200-250 million
Ans. Ⓒ 110-130 million

Q-30. What was the name given to load deeds in the Mughal period?
Ans. Dastawez

Culture during the Mughal Empire: Persian Literature (including Historical Works). Hindi and Religious Literatures. Mughal Architecture, Mughal Painting, Provincial Schools of architecture and Painting, Classical Music, Science and Technology. Sawai Jai Singh, an Astronomer, Mystic Eclecticism : Dara Shukoh, Vaishnav Bhakti, Maharashtra Dharma. Evolution of the Sikh Community (Khalsa)

Q-1. It is said that Akbar, Jahangir and Shah Jahan brought about the ____ of the Persian poetry.
- **A** Spring
- **B** Summer
- **C** Autumn
- **D** Winter

Ans. B Summer

Q-2. What was the distinct Indian style of the Persian poetry called?
Ans. Sabk-e-Hind

Q-3. How many poets in Akbar's court does the Ain-i-Akbari mention?
Ans. 59

Q-4. Who translated the Bhagavata Purana into Persian?
Ans. Todar Mal

Quiz Time History

Q-5. What was the name of Abul Fazl's collection of personal letters?
Ans. Raqqat

Q-6. _____'s son, Dara Shukoh translated some of the Upanishads.
- **A** Akbar
- **B** Babur
- **C** Shah Jahan
- **D** Jahangir

Ans. C Shah Jahan

Q-7. Who authored the Hindi classic "Padmavat"?
Ans. Malik Muhammad Jayasi

Q-8. Persian was the court language during the Mughal period, but what was the religious language?
Ans. Arabic

Q-9. _____ marble was used for most architectural constructions during Shah Jahan's reign.
- **A** White
- **B** Black
- **C** Speckled
- **D** Yellow

Ans A White

Q-10. Which fort is famous for the Diwan-e-aam and Diwan-e-khas?
Ans. Red Fort

Q-11. How many storeys does the Qutub Minar have?
Ans. Five

Q-12. Which of these was not used to construct the Qutub Minar?
- **A** Grey quartzite
- **B** Red sandstone
- **C** Brick
- **D** Marble

Ans. C Brick

Early and Medieval Indian History

Q-13. The Panch Mahal in Fatehpur Sikri resembles a _____ vihara.
- Ⓐ Buddhist
- Ⓑ Hindu
- Ⓒ Christian
- Ⓓ Jain

Ans. Ⓐ Buddhist

Q-14. Which ruler was called the "Prince of Builders"?
Ans. Shah Jahan

Q-15. The Jama Masjid is the largest mosque in _____.
- Ⓐ Asia
- Ⓑ The world
- Ⓒ Delhi
- Ⓓ India

Ans. Ⓓ India

Jama Masjid

Q-16. Name two famous painters during Akbar's rule.
Ans. Basawan and Daswant

Q-17. Which art series shows the difference of the style between Mir Sayyid Ali and Abdul Samad?
Ans. Hamza Namah series

Quiz Time History

Q-18. Which Mughal ruler terminated all painting activity in the court as he believed it was anti-Islamic?
Ans. Aurangzeb

Q-19. Arabesque is a type of _____.
  Ⓐ Artistic design   Ⓑ Paint
  Ⓒ Tool   Ⓓ Glue
Ans. Ⓐ Artistic design

Q-20. Into how many classes are musical instruments categorised in the Ain-i-Akbari?
Ans. Four

Q-21. What unique instrument was created during the Mughal period that had to be played by nine musicians at the same time?
Ans. Naubat

Q-22. What is the famous observatory in Delhi built by Sawai Jai Singh?
Ans. Jantar Mantar

Q-23. Which Sikh Guru did Dara Shikoh strike a deep friendship with?
Ans. Guru Har Rai

Q-24. Name Dara Shikoh's most famous work about Sufi and Vedantic mysticism.
Ans. Majma-ul-Bahrain or The Confluence of Two Seas

Q-25. What is the other name for the five different moods of the Vaishnava Bhakti tradition?
Ans. Bhavas

Q-26. Which temple was the centre of the Bhakti Movement in Maharashtra?
Ans. Vitthoba or Vittal

Q-27. Who authored Dasbodha?
Ans. Ramdas

Q-28. What are the five K's of the Khalsa that form their uniform?
Ans. Kes (hair), Kanga (comb), Karra (bracelet), Kachera (Undergarments) and Kirpan (dagger)

Q-29. Who is the "Mother" of the Khalsa?
Ans. Mata Sahib Kaur

Q-30. What script is the Adi Grath or Guru Granth Sahib composed in?
Ans. Gurmukhi script

First Half of 18th Century: Factors Behind Decline of the Mughal Empire. The Regional Principalities (Nizam's Deccan, Bengal, Awadh). Rise of Maratha Ascendancy under the Peshwas. The Maratha Fiscal and Financial System. Emergence of Afghan Power, Panipat, 1761. Internal Weaknesses: Political, Cultural and Economic, on the eve of the British Conquest

Q-1. The _____ policy of Aurangzeb was one of the major reasons for Mughal decline.
- **A** Northern
- **B** Deccan
- **C** Eastern
- **D** Slave

Ans. **B** Deccan

Q-2. Where did the Turanis originally come from?
Ans. Transoxiana

Q-3. A popular saying of the time, "Takht ya taboot" reflected the violent struggle of succession at the end of every reign. What did it mean?
Ans. Throne or Coffin

Q-4. After whose invasion in 1739 AD did the Mughal Empire almost cease to exist as an Indian political unit?
Ans. Nadir Shah

Early and Medieval Indian History

Q-5. Which Persian Shia adventurer was made the governor of Awadh in 1722 AD?
Ans. Saadat Khan

Q-6. With which two Maratha chiefs did Abul Mansur Khan Safdarjung create an alliance with?
Ans. Jayappa Sindhia and Malhar Rao Holkar

Q-7. Who was granted the governorship of Orissa in 1719 AD by the emperor, Farukh Siyar?
Ans. Murshid Quli Khan

Q-8. Who legalised his usurpation by exchanging two crores for a *farman* from the Emperor?
Ans. Alivardi Khan

Q-9. Which two places did Siraj ud-Daulah seize in 1756 AD when the English didn't comply?
Ans. Kasimbazar and Calcutta (Kolkata)

Q-10. On which day did the Black Hole Episode take place?
Ans. 20 June, 1756

Q-11. What was the name of Shivaji's grandson who was released from captivity after Aurangzeb's death?
Ans. Sahu

Q-12. In which year did Raja Ram die?
Ans. 1700 AD

Q-13. Whom did Sahu appoint as his Peshwa or Prime Minister?
Ans. Balaji Vishwanath

Q-14. What was "Chauth"?
- Ⓐ Tax
- Ⓑ Land
- Ⓒ Grains
- Ⓓ Gold

Ans. Ⓐ Tax

Quiz Time History

Q-15. In which year did Balaji Vishwanath sign a significant treaty with the Sayyid brothers that broke the invincibility of Mughal power?
Ans. 1714 AD

Q-16. Peshwa Baji Rao I was Balaji Vishwanath's _____.
- **A** Brother
- **B** Grandson
- **C** Father
- **D** Son

Ans. D Son

Q-17. Which Mughal Emperor was compelled to sign the Treaty of Sironj after Balaji Rao defeated the Mughal forces in 1737 AD?
Ans. Mohammad Shah

Q-18. Which ruler battled the Marathas in the Third Battle of Panipat?
Ans. Ahmed Shah Abdali

Q-19. Name the five kingdoms created after the breakup of the Maratha confederacy.
Ans. Bhonsle, Gaikwad, Holkar, Sindhia and Satara

Q-20. Sardeshmukhi was a tax of ____ on the total revenue that was exacted by Shivaji.
- **A** 1/6th
- **B** 1/10th
- **C** 1/5th
- **D** 1/3rd

Ans. B 1/10th

Q-21. What was the scale used to measure land during the time of Shivaji?
Ans. Kathi

Q-22. How old was Ahmed Shah Abdali's son, Timur when his father appointed him as the *subedar* of Lahore?
Ans. 13 years old

Early and Medieval Indian History

Timur

Q-23. Name Aurangzeb's three living sons at the time of his death.
Ans. Muazzam, Azam and Kam Baksh

Q-24. Whose banking house became very popular under the reign of Alivardi Khan?
Ans. Jagat Seth

Q-25. Which governor of Awadh tried to reduce the number of *jagirdars* appointed by the Mughals?
Ans. Saadat Khan

Q-26. Hyder Ali started his career in the ____ army.
 Ⓐ Punjab   Ⓑ Awadh
 Ⓒ Mysore   Ⓓ Bengal
Ans. Ⓒ Mysore

Q-27. How many times did Ahmed Shah Abdali invade India between 1748 AD and 1761 AD?
Ans. Five times

Q-28. Which Nawab supported Ahmed Shah Abdali in the Third Battle of Panipat?
Ans. Rohila Nawab of Oudh

Quiz Time History

Q-29. Who was the eighth and last Maratha Peshwa?
Ans. Baji Rao II

Q-30. Who commanded the Maratha artillery in the Third Battle of Panipat?
Ans. Ibrahim Khan Gardi

Modern Indian History and Contemporary World History

Establishment of British Rule in India: Factors Behind British Success Against Indian Powers-Mysore, Maratha Confederacy and the Punjab as Major Powers in Resistance; Policy of Subsidiary Alliance and Doctrine of Lapse

Q-1. Which treaty was signed after the 2nd Carnatic War?
Ans. The Treaty of Pondicherry

Q-2. Which Frenchman was defeated in The Battle of Wandiwash in 1760?
Ans. Count de Lally

Q-3. Which treaty signed in 1763 sealed the British supremacy in India?
Ans. The Treaty of Paris

Q-4. Which Nawab stopped the illegal private trade that the British were carrying out after their *farman* was granted in 1717?
Ans. Mir Qasim

Q-5. Who led the English in the Battle of Buxar?
Ans. Munro

Q-6. In which year was Robert Clive appointed the governor of Bengal for the second time?
Ans. 1765

Q-7. Who was the ruler of Mysore in 1761?
Ans. Haider Ali

Q-8. Which Nizam supported Haider Ali in the First Anglo-Mysore war?
Ans. Nizam of Hyderabad

Q-9. Tipu Sultan was Haider Ali's ____.
  Ⓐ Son   Ⓑ Brother
  Ⓒ Grandson   Ⓓ Uncle
Ans. Ⓐ Son

Tipu Sultan

Q-10. Which Governor-General signed the Treaty of Seringapatnam in 1792?
Ans. Lord Cornwallis

Q-11. When the Marathas tried to seize Delhi, the British supported ____ in resisting them.
  Ⓐ Bengal   Ⓑ Mewar
  Ⓒ Awadh   Ⓓ Punjab
Ans. Ⓒ Awadh

Q-12. The first Anglo-Maratha war started when Raghunath Rao killed the ruling Peshwa. Name the Peshwa.
Ans; Peshwa Narayan Rao

Q-13. In which year was the Treaty of Surat signed?
Ans. 1775

Q-14. Who was recognised as Maharaja after the Treaty of Lahore?
Ans. Dalip Singh

Q-15. In which year did the Sikhs surrender at Rawalpindi?
Ans. 1849

Q-16. Under whose reign did the subsidiary alliance fully develop?
Ans. Lord Wellesley

Q-17. Under whose Governor-Generalship did the Nawab of Oudh agree not to employ any European in Oudh?
Ans. Sir John Shore

Q-18. In which year did the British change their previous stance and state that the Government had the right to accept or reject the adopted heir nominated by a ruler?
Ans. 1831

Q-19. Into how many categories did Lord Dalhousie divide the Indian states?
Ans. Three

Q-20. After the death of Raja Gangadhar Rao, his widow fought bravely for the right of her adopted son. Name the widow.
Ans. Rani Lakshmi Bai

Colonial Economy : Tribute System, Drain of Wealth and "deindustrialisation", Fiscal Pressures and Revenue Settlements (Zamindari, Ryotwari and Mahalwari Settlements); Structure of the British Raj up to 1857 (including the Acts of 1773 and 1784 and Administrative Organisation)

Q-1. Who was the first person to expose the "drain of wealth" concept through his paper, "English debt to India"?
Ans. Dadabhai Naoroji

Q-2. Name one "visible" form of drain of wealth?
Ans. Gifts, bribes, or profits earned through "Dastak" (Any one)

Q-3. Economists have argued that the drain was not only a loss of wealth, but also a loss of ____.
- **Ⓐ** People
- **Ⓑ** Land
- **Ⓒ** Capital
- **Ⓓ** Gold

Ans. Ⓒ Capital

Q-4. In which year did the English government pass an act that involved banning cloth imports from India?
Ans. 1700

Q-5. Which act of 1813 ended the monopoly of the East India Company except in tea and trade with China?
Ans. The Charter Act

Quiz Time History

Q-6. In 1720 England, a penalty of ___ pounds was imposed on those who wore Indian silk or calicos.
- Ⓐ 5
- Ⓑ 20
- Ⓒ 25
- Ⓓ 30

Ans. Ⓐ 5

Q-7. Which European nation did not adopt the protectionist policy against Indian goods?
Ans. (Holland) The Netherlands

Q-8. What was the other name of the Zamindari System?
Ans. Permanent Settlement

Q-9. In 1786, what kind of settlement did the Court of Directors urge Lord Cornwallis to make with the Zamindars?
Ans. Decennial Settlement

Lord Cornwallis

Q-10. What percentage of British India did the Permanent Settlement cover?
Ans. About 19 percent

Q-11. According to the Permanent Settlement, what percentage of collected rent did the State claim?
Ans. Around 89 percent

Q-12. In which year was the Bengal Tenancy Act passed?
Ans. 1859

Q-13. Who was the main Britisher behind the Ryotwari Settlement?
Ans. Thomas Munro

Q-14. What does the word "Ryot" mean in Persian?
Ans. Peasant

Q-15. Although the Mahalwari Settlement was legally sanctioned in 1822, when did it fully develop?
Ans. 1833-34

Q-16. With the passing of The Regulating Act of 1773, who was named the Governor-General of Bengal?
Ans. Warren Hastings

Q-17. Which act of 1784 reduced the members of the Executive Council to three from four?
Ans. Pitt's India Act

Q-18. Who kept all the Indians out of the civil services, which he introduced in 1793?
Ans. Lord Cornwallis

Q-19. What was the highest court of appeal for criminal cases?
Ans. Sadar Nizamat

Q-20. In which period was William Bentinck the Governor-General?
Ans. 1828-35

Resistance to Colonial rule: Early Uprisings; Causes, Nature and Impact of the Revolt of 1857; Reorganisation of the Raj, 1858 and After

Q-1. The revolt broke out on the issue of _____ cartridges.
- Ⓐ Black
- Ⓑ Greased
- Ⓒ Poisoned
- Ⓓ Dirty

Ans. Ⓑ Greased

Q-2. In which year did the 38th Naval infantry refuse to go to Burma?
Ans. 1852

Q-3. Which Nawab of Awadh was accused of misgovernance?
Ans. Nawab Wajid Ali Shah

Q-4. The Company stopped the annual pension of the adopted son of the last Peshwa Baji Rao II. Name the son.
Ans. Nana Sahib

Peshwa Baji Rao II

Modern Indian History and Contemporary World History

Q-5. In which year was English made the national language?
Ans. 1835

Q-6. Which act passed in 1850, allowed a converted person to inherit property?
Ans. Religious Disabilities Act

Q-7. After firing on their officers, the soldiers of Meerut crossed the Yamuna and destroyed the southern gate of the ___ Fort.
- (A) Red
- (B) Old
- (C) Meerut
- (D) Mewar

Ans. (A) Red

Q-8. Who was the official Mughal Commander-in-chief during the revolt?
Ans. Mirza Mughal

Q-9. Which *havaldar* of the Bareilly force was the real leader?
Ans. Muhammad Bakhtawar Khan

Q-10. Which Begum led the revolt in Lucknow?
Ans. Begum Hazrat Mahal

Q-11. Who supported Nana Sahib when he led the movement from Kanpur?
Ans. Tantya Tope

Q-12. Which British commander of the garrison surrendered on 27 June?
Ans. Sri Hugh Wheeler

Q-13. In which year did Rani Lakshmi Bai of Jhansi die while fighting bravely?
Ans. 1858

Quiz Time History

Q-14. Who led the revolt at Patna?
Ans. Maulvi Pir Ali

Q-15. Which ruler was more concerned about his and his wife Zeenat Mahal's safety rather than the revolt?
Ans. Bahadur Shah Zafar

Q-16. Did the educated middle class participate in the revolt?
Ans. No

Q-17. What ratio was maintained in the Bengal army between Europeans and Indians after the revolt?
Ans. 1:2

Q-18. In which year was the East India Association formed?
Ans. 1866

Q-19. Who was the first Indian to write about the revolt?
Ans. Sir Syed Ahmed Khan

Q-20. Which British Prime Minister introduced the "Bill for Better Government of India"?
Ans. Lord Palmerston

Q-21. Which Act brought the end of the East India Company's rule?
Ans. The Government of India Act

Q-22. To whom were the powers of the Court of Director and Board of Control transferred?
Ans. The Secretary of State

Q-23. The council of the Secretary of State had ____ members.
- Ⓐ 10
- Ⓑ 12
- Ⓒ 8
- Ⓓ 15

Ans. ⓘ 15

Q-24. In which year was the first Indian Council Act passed?
Ans. 1861

Q-25. Who was the Governor-General of India between 1884 and 1888?
Ans. Lord Dufferin

Socio-cultural Impact of Colonial Rule: Official Social Reform Measures (1828-57); Orientalist-Anglicist Controversy; Coming of English Education and the Press; Christian Missionary Activities; Bengal Renaissance; Social and Religious Reform Movements in Bengal and Other Areas; Women as Focus of Social Reform

Q-1. Who passed a resolution in 1829 that declared Sati as "culpable homicide" or "suicide"?
Ans. Lord William Bentinck

Q-2. Which act did Lord Harding I ban which was mostly prevalent amongst the Gonds?
Ans. Human sacrifice

Q-3. In which year were the Women Disability Act and the Widow Remarriage Act passed?
Ans. 1856

Q-4. Who wrote in favour of the widow remarriage in Tattva Bodhini?
Ans. Ishwar Chandra Vidyasagar

Q-5. What were Muslim primary schools called?
Ans. Maktab

Q-6. In which year was the Calcutta Madrasa established?
Ans. 1781

Q-7. Who founded the Benares Sanskrit College in 1791?
Ans. Jonathan Duncan

Q-8. Which college was started in Calcutta for the instruction of English civil servants of the Company?
Ans. Fort William College

Q-9. In which year did the Governor-General in Council appoint a General Committee on Public Instruction for the Presidency of Bengal?
Ans. 1823

Q-10. Which two groups were the members of the General Committee on Public Instruction divided into?
Ans. Orientalist and Anglicist

Q-11. Which group did James Prinsep and H. H. Wilson belong to?
Ans. Orientalist group

Q-12. In which year was Persian abolished and English adopted as the court language?
Ans. 1837

Q-13. In which year was The Indian University Act passed?
Ans. 1904

Q-14. What was the first newspaper in India?
Ans. *The Bengal Gazette* or *Calcutta General Advertiser*

Q-15. Who was the first Indian to start publishing newspapers in Indian languages?
Ans. Raja Rammohan Roy

Quiz Time History

Q-16. Which censorship act did Lord Wellesley pass in 1799?
Ans. The Censorship of Press Act

Q-17. Who set up a missionary establishment in Serampore?
Ans. Sir William Carey

Q-18. What was another name of the Serampore Mission?
Ans. The Baptist Missionary Society

Q-19. In which place did the London Missionary Society set up a girl's college in 1818?
Ans. Chinsura

Q-20. From whom did Raja Rammohan Roy learn Tantricism at Rangpur?
Ans; Hariharananda Tirthaswamy

Raja Rammohan Roy

Q-21. In which year was the Brahmo Samaj founded?
Ans. 1828

Q-22. What did "Kulinism" mean?
Ans. Polygamy

Q-23. What was Raja Rammohan Roy's first book?
Ans. *Tuhfat-ul-Muwahhidin* or *A gift to monotheist*

Q-24. Who founded the Goodwill Fraternity?
Ans. Keshab Chandra Sen

Q-25. What was Swami Vivekananda's original name?
Ans. Narendranath Dutta

Q-26. Where was the Ramakrishna Mission set up in 1897?
Ans. Belur

Q-27. In which year was the Prarthna Samaj founded in Bombay (Mumbai)?
Ans. 1867

Q-28. Who is remembered as the Father of Renaissance in western India?
Ans. Mahadev Govind Ranade

Economy: 1858-1914, Railways; Commercialisation of Indian Agriculture; Growth of Landless Labourers and Rural Indebtedness, Famines; India as Market for British Industry; Customs Removal, Exchange and countervailing Excise; Limited Growth of Modern Industry

Q-1. What percent excise duty did the British impose on the Indian textile industry?
Ans. About 5 percent

Q-2. Which system was extremely exploitative and harmful for the growth of Indian agriculture?
Ans. The Zamindari System

Q-3. The opening of which canal reduced the journey time between Britain and India to three weeks?
Ans. Suez Canal

Q-4. Between 1902 and 1913, India met nearly one-fifth of Britain's demand for ____.
    Ⓐ Cotton   **Ⓑ** Indigo
    Ⓒ Wheat   **Ⓓ** Textiles
Ans. Ⓒ Wheat

Q-5. Which beverage item did India export to Britain?
Ans. Tea

Modern Indian History and Contemporary World History

Q-6. In which year did Asia's first steam-powered cotton mill open in India?
Ans. 1856

Q-7. Where did the first steam-powered jute mill open?
Ans. Calcutta, presently called Kolkata.

Q-8. Between 1908 and 1942 ____ famines occurred in India.
  Ⓐ 8   Ⓑ No major
  Ⓒ 6   Ⓓ 18
Ans. Ⓑ No major

Q-9. In which year was the first experimental railway line started from Bombay to Thane?
Ans. 1853

Q-10. Who drafted the famous Railway Minute in 1853 that became the guideline book for all upcoming railway projects in India?
Ans. Lord Dalhousie

Q-11. Where was the first Indian railway engine built in 1865?
Ans. Bombay, presently known as Mumbai.

Q-12. In which year did the peasants belonging to the Deccan highlands attack the Marwari moneylenders?
Ans. 1875

Q-13. How many shillings was a silver Indian rupee worth in 1872?
Ans. 2 shillings

Indian rupee notes and coins

Quiz Time History

Q-14. Despite the crisis during the Afghan war, which lobby in Britain refused to allow India to raise custom duties?
Ans. The Lancashire Lobby

Q-15. Which Viceroy allowed Indians a certain amount of say in local affairs in 1882?
Ans. Lord Ripon

Q-16. In which year were the Morley-Minto Reforms declared?
Ans. 1909

Q-17. The ___ Tenancy Act was passed in 1885.
- **Ⓐ** Punjab
- **Ⓑ** Lahore
- **Ⓒ** Bengal
- **Ⓓ** Deccan

Ans. Ⓒ Bengal

Q-18. In which three cities were provincial councils created after the Indian Councils Act of 1861?
Ans. Calcutta, Madras and Bombay

Early Indian Nationalism: Social Background; Formation of National Associations; Peasant and Tribal Uprising during the Early Nationalist Era; Foundation of the Indian National Congress (INC); The Moderate Phase of the Congress; Growth of Extremism; The Indian Council Act of 1909; Home Rule Movement; The Government of India Act of 1919.

Q-1. Who founded the Aryan Samaj?
Ans. Swami Dayananda Saraswati

Q-2. In which year was the British Indian Association started?
Ans. 1851

Q-3. Who founded the Indian National Congress (INC)?
Ans. A. O. Hume

Q-4. What did the Congress demand the age for taking competitive exams be increased to?

- Ⓐ 17
- Ⓑ 23
- Ⓒ 25
- Ⓓ 18

Ans. Ⓑ 23

Quiz Time History

Q-5. In 1888, under who's leadership was a paid Indian Agency set up?
Ans. William Digby

Q-6. In which year was the Indian Parliamentary Committee formed?
Ans. 1893

Q-7. The partition of which state changed the course of the freedom struggle and started the extremist movement?
Ans. Bengal

People protesting after the Bengal partition

Q-8. What were the three main slogans used during this extremist period?
Ans. Swaraj, Swadeshi and Boycott

Q-9. In which year did the Surat split take place in the Congress?
Ans. 1907

Modern Indian History and Contemporary World History

Q-10. Which separatist body did the British encourage and allow to be founded in December 1906?
Ans. All-India Muslim League

Q-11. In which state did *Abhinava Bharat* make its presence strongly felt?
Ans. Maharashtra

Q-12. Which association did Ajit Singh and Syed Hyder Riza form, taking advantage of the discontent after the Colonisation Bill?
Ans. Indian Patriots Association

Q-13. Who was the Secretary of State at the time of The August Declaration?
Ans. Lord Montague

Q-14. Which peasant movement abolished the Tinkathia System?
Ans. Champaran Satyagraha

Q-15. Which two people established Home Rule Leagues in 1916?
Ans. Bal Gangadhar Tilak and Mrs Annie Besant

Q-16. Who set up the newspapers, *New India*, *Commonwealth* and *Young India*?
    Ⓐ Bal Gangadhar Tilak   Ⓑ Subramanian Iyer
    Ⓒ Annie Besant   Ⓓ Gandhiji
Ans. Ⓒ Annie Besant

Q-17. On the basis of which report was the Government of India Act passed in 1919?
Ans. Montague-Chelmsford Report

Q-18. What were the rules made under the Government of India Act known as?

Ans. Devolution rules

Q-19. Which two categories were the subjects of administration divided into by the Government of India Act?

Ans. Central and Provincial categories.

Q-20. Which two parties signed the Lucknow Pact in 1916?
- **Ⓐ** Britain and Indian National Congress
- **Ⓑ** Indian National Congress and Muslim league
- **Ⓒ** Britain and Muslim League
- **Ⓓ** Extremists and Moderates

Ans. **Ⓑ** Indian National Congress and Muslim League

Inter-War Economy of India: Industries and Problem of Protection, Agricultural Distress, the Great Depression; Ottawa Agreements and Discriminatory Protection; the Growth of Trade Unions; The Kisan Movement; The Economic Programme of the Congress, the Karachi Resolution, 1931

Q-1. In which year did the Royal Commission on Agriculture make its recommendations excluding the topics of land revenue and tenancy?
Ans. 1926

Q-2. After 1919, the Central Department of Agriculture concerned itself with ____ agricultural issues.
    Ⓐ All India   **Ⓑ** Northern states
    Ⓒ Southern states   **Ⓓ** No
Ans. **Ⓐ** All India

Q-3. Which ten years did the agriculturists suffer through during the Great Depression?
Ans. 1929 to 1939

Q-4. Which act restrained the powers of moneylenders during this period?
Ans. The Moneylenders' Act

Quiz Time History

Q-5. Which conference in 1942 proposed to increase the production of food grains?
Ans. Food Production Conference

Q-6. What principle was the Ottawa Trade Agreement of 1932 based on?
Ans. Imperial Preference

Q-7. By the Ottawa Trade Agreement, the United Kingdom gave free entry to all Indian commodities falling within the schedule bearing _____ % duty under the Import Duty Act.
- **A** 8
- **B** 12
- **C** 10
- **D** 9

Ans. C 10

Q-8. According to the Ottawa Trade Agreement, India granted 7.5% preference on certain classes of _____.
- **A** Textiles
- **B** Hard metals
- **C** Electrical equipment
- **D** Motor vehicles

Ans. D Motor vehicles

Q-9. In which year was the Mody-Lees Pact signed?
Ans. 1933

Q-10. Which Agreement was made in 1935 as a supplementary to the Ottawa Trade Agreement?
Ans. The Indo-British Trade Agreement

Q-11. What is the full form of AITUC?
Ans. The All India Trade Union Congress

Q-12. In which year did ideological differences cause a split in the AITUC?
Ans. 1929

Modern Indian History and Contemporary World History

Q-13. Which important Act passed in 1926 allowed for voluntary registration and gave rights to the registered trade unions in return for following certain obligations?
Ans. The Trade Union Act

Q-14. In which year did the NTUF and the AITUC become affiliated?
Ans. 1938

Q-15. Which organisation was set up in 1920 under the leadership of Pandit Jawaharlal Nehru and Gauri Shankar Misra to protect the peasant rights?
Ans. Oudh Kisan Sabha

Pandit Jawaharlal Nehru

Q-16. Who established the Kisan Sabha in Bihar?
Ans. Swami Sahajanand Saraswati

Q-17. Who led the no-revenue campaign that was against a revenue hike in Bardoli by the Bombay government?
Ans. Sardar Vallabhbhai Patel

Q-18. Which pact did the Congress meeting at Karachi in 1931 endorse?
Ans. The Gandhi-Irwin Pact or the Delhi Pact

Q-19. Who drafted the Fundamental Rights and National Economic Programme?
Ans. Dr. Rajendra Prasad

Q-20. Which famous revolutionary was executed six days before the Karachi resolution?
Ans. Bhagat Singh

Nationalism under Gandhi's leadership: Gandhi's Career, Thought and Methods of Mass Mobilisation; Rowlatt Satyagraha, Khilafat- Non-Cooperation Movement, Civil Disobedience Movement, 1940 Satyagraha and Quit India Movement; State People's Movement

Q-1. In which year did Gandhiji enter the political scene in India with Satyagraha in Champaran, Bihar?
Ans. 1917

Gandhiji

Q-2. Which act allowed the Government to imprison any person without trial or conviction?
Ans. Rowlatt Act

Q-3. On which date did the Khilafat Committee launch a Non-Cooperation Movement?
Ans. 31 August 1920

Q-4. Which fund was started to finance the Non-Cooperation Movement?
Ans. Tilak Swaraj Fund

Q-5. Which violent incident led Gandhiji to suspend the Non-Cooperation Movement in 1922?
Ans. Chauri Chaura incident

Q-6. In which session did the Indian National Congress (INC) declare that their political goal was independence for India?
Ans. Madras/Chennai Session

Q-7. Which famous march marked the beginning of the Civil Disobedience Movement?
Ans. Dandi or Salt March

Q-8. Who was the leader of *Rashtriya Stree Sangha*?
Ans. Sarojini Naidu

Q-9. What was the slogan Gandhiji gave for the Quit India Movement?
Ans. Do or die

Q-10. On which date did the Quit India Movement begin?
Ans. 8 August 1942

Q-11. During this time which secret radio station broadcasted anti-colonial messages?
Ans. Congress Radio

Q-12. Which "children of God" was Gandhiji particularly passionate about empowering?
Ans. Harijans

Q-13. What is the meaning of the word 'satyagraha'?
Ans. 'Hold fast the truth'

Q-14. In which year did Gandhiji take over Annie Besant's Home Rule League?
Ans. 1920

Q-15. What common commodity did Gandhiji encourage people to make themselves so that tax on it could be avoided?
Ans. Salt

Q-16. Who became the President of the All India States' People's Conference in 1935?
Ans. Pandit Jawaharlal Nehru

Q-17. Who first gave Gandhiji the name "Mahatma"?
Ans. Rabindranath Tagore

Q-18. In which year did Gandhiji assume leadership of the Indian National Congress (INC)?
Ans. 1921

Q-19. In the summer of which year were three assassination attempts made on Gandhiji's life?
Ans. 1934

Q-20. Which famous Dalit leader initially showed suspicion towards Gandhiji?
Ans. Dr. B. R. Ambedkar

Other Strands of the National Movement: a) Revolutionary Movements since 1905; (b) Constitutional Politics; Swarajists, Liberals, Responsive Cooperation; (c) Ideas of Jawharlal Nehru, (d) The Left (Socialists and Communists); (e) Subhas Chandra Bose and the Indian National Army (INA); (f) Communal Strands: Muslim League and Hindu Mahasabha; (g) Women in the National Movement

Q-1. Which pair of brothers from Poona assassinated two British officials in 1897?
Ans. Chapekar Brothers

Q-2. Which secret society did Ganesh Sarvarkar start in 1907?
Ans. Abhinava Bharat

Q-3. Who was the leader of the Chittagong group of revolutionaries?
Ans. Surya Sen

Q-4. In which year did C. R. Das formally announce the formation of a new party within the Congress?
Ans; 1923

Quiz Time History

Q-5. In the general elections in 1923, which party gained a huge majority in Bengal, United Provinces, Bombay and Assam?
Ans. Swaraj Party

Q-6. Which committee was set up by the government to inquire into the working of the Reforms of 1919?
Ans. Muddiman Committee

Q-7. Who convinced Nehru to make India join the Non-Aligned Movement?
Ans. Krishna Menon

Q-8. In which year did Nehru draw up the first Five-Year Plan?
Ans. 1951

Q-9. Nehru believed in and worked towards a ____ economy system.
- Ⓐ Single
- Ⓑ Dual
- Ⓒ Mixed
- Ⓓ Flat

Ans. Ⓒ Mixed

Q-10. In which year did the government ban the Communist Party of India?
Ans. 1934

Q-11. Which new party, affiliated to the Congress did the communists approve of?
Ans. Congress Socialist Party

Q-12. In which year was the All India Students' Federation started?
Ans. 1936

Q-13. In the Calcutta Congress of 1928, what did Netaji Subhas Chandra Bose demand instead of "dominion status"?
Ans. Complete independence

Modern Indian History and Contemporary World History

Q-14. What was the other name for the INA or Indian National Army?
Ans. Azad Hind Fauj

Q-15. How many times had Netaji Subhas Chandra Bose been arrested before his house arrest in 1940?
    Ⓐ 10   Ⓑ 12
    Ⓒ 15   Ⓓ 6
Ans. Ⓐ 10

The INA

Q-16. After Jinnah parted ways with the Congress, all Muslim groups came together and signed a single document called Jinnah's ___ Point Programme.
    Ⓐ 5   Ⓑ 14
    Ⓒ 11   Ⓓ 20
Ans. Ⓑ 14

Q-17. Who presided over the 1930 session of the Muslim League and said he would like to see "Punjab, North-western frontier provinces, Sind and Baluchistan amalgamated into a single state"?
Ans. Mohammad Iqbal

Q-18. Where was the first All India Hindu Mahasabha Conference held?
Ans. Haridwar

Q-19. Who was the first Indian woman to hold a ministerial rank?
Ans. Vijayalakshmi Pandit

Q-20. Which three women led the *Desh Sevika Sangh*?
Ans. Kamala Nehru, Kasturba Gandhi and Sarojini Naidu

Literary and Cultural Movements: Tagore, Premchand, Subramanyam Bharati, Iqbal as examples only; New Trends in Art; Film Industry; Writers' Organisations and Theatre Associations

Q-1. Who composed the Indian national anthem?
Ans. Rabindranath Tagore

Q-2. For which work did Tagore win the Nobel Prize for Literature in 1913?
Ans. Gitanjali

Q-3. Which play by Dinabandhu Mitra depicted the atrocities of the indigo planters through drama?
Ans. Neel Darpan

Q-4. In which year was the first gramophone company of India formed?
Ans. 1902

Q-5. Which British painter introduced India to oil painting?
Ans. Tilly Kettle

Q-6. Who composed "*Saare Jahaan se accha*"?
Ans. Muhammad Iqbal

Q-7. Who is known as the "Father of Indian Cinema"?
Ans. Dadasaheb Phalke

Modern Indian History and Contemporary World History

Q-8. What is the full form of IPTA that was established in 1942?
Ans. Indian People's Theatre Association

Q-9. After the publication of which collection of short stories was the Indian Progressive Writers' Movement and Association started?
Ans. *Angare*

Q-10. In which year was the Indian Progressive Writers' Association set up in London?
Ans. 1935

Q-11. Which famous writer has been called "Upanyas Samrat"?
Ans. Munshi Premchand

Q-12. Premchand was elected as the _____ President of the Progressive Writers' Association in Lucknow.
    Ⓐ Third   Ⓑ First
    Ⓒ Last   Ⓓ Second
Ans. Ⓑ First

Q-13. Who was popularly known as Mahakavi Bharathiyar?
Ans. Subramanya Bharathi

Q-14. Where did Subramanya Bharathi flee in 1908 after the government issued an arrest warrant against him?
Ans. Pondicherry

Q-15. Sister Nivedita regarded herself to be the _____ of Swami Vivekananda.
    Ⓐ Teacher   Ⓑ Relative
    Ⓒ Spiritual daughter   Ⓓ Guide
Ans. Ⓒ Spiritual daughter

Quiz Time History

Sister Nivedita

Q-16. Who wrote the play, *Congress Vijayam*?
Ans. Jasti Venkata Narasayya

Q-17. Which famous IPTA play told the story of Bengali peasants during the 1943 famine?
Ans. *Navanna* or *New Harvest*

Q-18. Which Act was also known as the "Gagging Act"?
Ans. Vernacular Press Act

Q-19. Which Bengali newspaper became an English-language paper to circumvent censorship?
Ans. *Amrita Bazaar Patrika*

Q-20. Name the famous Urdu poet who was knighted by King George V in 1922.
Ans. Muhammad Iqbal

Towards Freedom: The Act of 1935; Congress Ministries, 1937-1939; The Pakistan Movement; Post-1945 Upsurge (RIN Mutiny, Telangana Uprising, etc.); Constitutional Negotiations and the Transfer of Power, 15 August 1947

Q-1. According to the Act of 1935, which two chambers were created within the Federal Legislature?
Ans. Federal Assembly and Council of State

Q-2. What kind of autonomy was introduced through the Act of 1935?
Ans. Provincial autonomy

Q-3. By the Act of 1935 which two legislative houses were created in Assam, Bengal, Bihar, Bombay, Madras and the United Provinces?
Ans. Legislative Council and Legislative Assembly

Q-4. In which of these provinces were Congress ministries not formed?
- Ⓐ Bombay
- Ⓑ Madras
- Ⓒ Bihar
- Ⓓ Bengal

Ans. Ⓓ Bengal

Q-5. In which year was there no session of the Congress?
Ans. 1937

Q-6. Although Netaji Subhas Chandra Bose won the election of the President of the Tripura session of the Congress, who was Gandhiji's candidate?
Ans. Pattabhi Sitaramayya

Netaji Subhas Chandra Bose

Q-7. Who was the Secretary of the Muslim League in 1937?
Ans. Liaquat Ali Khan

Q-8. In which year did the All-India Muslim League adopt the "Pakistan" resolution, recommending the partition?
Ans. 1940

Q-9. Whom did Winston Churchill send to India in 1942 to discuss the Draft Declaration?
Ans. Sir Stafford Cripps

Q-10. The other name for the RIN or Royal Indian Navy mutiny was the _____ mutiny.
- Ⓐ Bengal
- Ⓑ Bombay
- Ⓒ Madras
- Ⓓ Bihar

Ans. Ⓑ Bombay

Modern Indian History and Contemporary World History

Q-11. Which three flags did the ships hoist together during the RIN mutiny?
Ans. Congress, Muslim League and Communist Party of India flags

Q-12. Name two places where the British garrisons faced revolts within the ranks of the British Indian Army during the RIN mutiny?
Ans. Pune and Madras (Chennai)

Q-13. In 1946, the _____ speaking regions of Hyderabad came to be known as Telangana.
- Ⓐ Tamil
- Ⓑ Telugu
- Ⓒ Kannada
- Ⓓ Urdu

Ans. Ⓑ Telugu

Q-14. In which year was the Telangana insurgency used as an excuse for the intervention of the Indian Army?
Ans. 1948

Q-15. With which state established in 1953, was Telangana merged?
Ans. Andhra

Q-16. Who replaced Lord Wavell to become the next Viceroy?
Ans. Lord Mountbatten

Q-17. According to the Mountbatten Plan, the provincial assemblies of which two states were to decide on the issue of partition?
Ans. Bengal and Punjab

Q-18. What was the Mountbatten Plan called after it was ratified in 1947 by the British Parliament?
Ans. Indian Independence Act

Quiz Time History

Q-19. Who was the last viceroy of independent India?
Ans. C. Rajagopalachari

Q-20. Pakistan became independent on ___ August 1947.
    Ⓐ 12   Ⓑ 13
    Ⓒ 14   Ⓓ 15
Ans. Ⓒ 14

First Phase of Independence (1947-64): Facing the Consequences of Partition; Gandhiji's Murder; Economic Dislocation; Integration of States; The Democratic Constitution, 1950; Agrarian Reforms; Building an Industrial Welfare State; Planning and Industrialisation; Foreign Policy of Non-alignment; Relations with Neighbours

Q-1. When was the Indian Council of Agricultural Research established?
Ans; 1929

Q-2. Which famous steel company was set up in Jamshedpur in 1907?
Ans. Tata Iron and Steel Company

Q-3. Where in Bombay was the Bhabha Atomic Research Centre set up?
Ans; Trombay

Q-4. Between which two nations was the Tashkent Agreement signed?
Ans. India and Pakistan

Quiz Time History

Q-5. The "Panchsheel" or Five Principles of Peaceful Co-existence was signed between India and _____.
    Ⓐ Pakistan   Ⓑ Britain
    Ⓒ China   Ⓓ Sri Lanka
Ans. Ⓒ China

Q-6. Who defined the objectives of India's foreign policy in 1949?
Ans. Jawaharlal Nehru

Q-7. Name two principles of India's foreign policy.
Ans. Non-alignment, anti-colonialism, peaceful co-existence, anti-racialism, promotion of international peace and security, economic development (any two)

Q-8. On which date was Gandhiji assassinated?
Ans. 30 January 1948

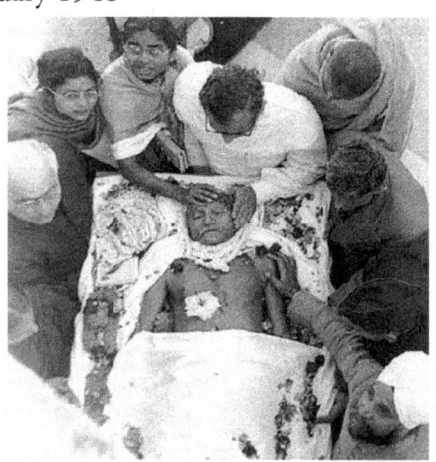

Gandhi's assassination/death

Q-9. In 1966, which Justice was appointed to inquire into the conspiracy of Gandhiji's murder?
Ans. Jivanlal Kapur

Modern Indian History and Contemporary World History

Q-10. The Indian constitution is the _____ written constitution of any sovereign country in the world.
- Ⓐ Longest
- Ⓑ 2nd longest
- Ⓒ 3rd longest
- Ⓓ Shortest

Ans. Ⓐ Longest

Q-11. Which two words were added to the constitutional definition of India in 1976 by a constitutional amendment?

Ans. Socialist and Secular

Q-12. On which day does India celebrate the adoption of the constitution?

Ans. 26 January or Republic Day

Q-13. Who was the first Home Minister of India?

Ans. Vallabhbhai Patel

Q-14. Which three states were not integrated with the Indian Union by 15 August 1947?

Ans. Junagadh, Hyderabad and Jammu and Kashmir

Q-15. During which time period was the second Five Year Plan executed?

Ans. 1956-1961

Q-16. Which bill was passed in 1955, which enforced monogamy on both men and women?

Ans. Hindu Code Bill

Q-17. In which year was an Indo-China Pact signed, which resulted in the Indian mission at Lahsa being given the status of a Super Commercial Embassy?

Ans. 1952

Q-18. Who visited the Indian Republic Day Parade in 1951 and praised the Indo-China friendship?

Ans. Mao tse Tung

Quiz Time History

Q-19. Who suggested the partition of Kashmir in 1950 when he was sent to demilitarise it?
Ans. Ovan Dixon

Q-20. By the Indian Independence Act of 1947, which post was abolished?
Ans. Secretary of State

Enlightenment and Modern Ideas
- ❑ Renaissance Background
- ❑ Major Ideas of Enlightenment: Kant, Rousseau
- ❑ Spread of Enlightenment outside Europe
- ❑ Rise of Socialist Ideas (to Marx)

Q-1. What does the French word "Renaissance" mean?
Ans. Rebirth

Q-2. The social ideal of a _____ person was propagated during the Renaissance.
- Ⓐ Single
- Ⓑ Universal
- Ⓒ Lonely
- Ⓓ Powerful

Ans. Ⓑ Universal

Q-3. Who is called The Father of Renaissance Humanism?
Ans. Petrarch

Q-4. Who was one of the first Italian humanists who learnt Greek and studied under Byzantine scholar Manuel Chrysoloras?
Ans. Leonardo Bruni

Q-5. Which three great artists make up the "High Renaissance" period?
Ans. Leonardo da Vinci, Raphael and Michelangelo

Quiz Time History

Famous artistic work from the Renaissance

Q-6. In Florence, who took control of the merchant oligarchy in 1434?

Ans. Cosimo de' Medici

Q-7. What new device created in 1446 made books more widely available?

Ans. Gutenberg movable type of printing press

Q-8. What work of Machiavelli got him ousted by the Medici?

Ans. The Prince

Q-9. What is Kant's most famous philosophical work?

Ans. Critique of Pure Reason

Q-10. Kant claimed to have created a _____ revolution in philosophy.

    Ⓐ Moral   Ⓑ Newtonian
    Ⓒ Transcendental   Ⓓ Copernican

Ans. Ⓓ Copernican

Q-11. Who propagated the "amour-propre" concept in philosophy?

Ans. Rousseau

Q-12. Which revolution was influenced by the political philosophy of Rousseau?
Ans. French Revolution

Q-13. Who was Marx's co-developer of the communist theory?
Ans. Friedrich Engels

Q-14. What was "diamat" in Marxist circles?
Ans. Dialectical materialism

Q-15. Which prince introduced Renaissance architecture to Russia by inviting Italian architects to his country?
Ans. Prince Ivan III

Q-16. The Age of Enlightenment sought to promote the power of _____.
   Ⓐ Reason   Ⓑ Religion
   Ⓒ Art   Ⓓ Morality
Ans. Ⓐ Reason

Q-17. Who is known as the "Father of Classical Liberalism"?
Ans. John Locke

Q-18. Who authored the posthumously published "Ethics"?
Ans. Baruch Spinoza

Q-19. Which famous scientist laid the foundation for most classical mechanics?
Ans. Sir Issac Newton

Q-20. Between which years was the Encyclopedie published in France?
Ans. 1751 and 1772

Origins of Modern Politics
- European States System
- American Revolution and the Constitution
- French Revolution and Aftermath, 1789-1815
- British Democratic Politics, 1815-1850; Parliamentary Reformers, Free Traders, Chartists

Q-1. What were Spanish Muslims known as?
Ans. Moriscos

Q-2. In which year did Charles V order his troops to invade Constantinople?
Ans. 1527

Q-3. Which two nations fought the 100 years war?
Ans. England and France

Q-4. The Holy League was created in 1571 to destroy the _____ control of the Eastern Mediterranean Sea.
- **Ⓐ** Ottoman Turks
- **Ⓑ** Turkish
- **Ⓒ** Spanish Armada
- **Ⓓ** English

Ans. Ⓐ Ottoman Turks

Q-5. Which series of peace treaties ended the Thirty Years' War?
Ans. Peace of Westphalia

Q-6. In the American Revolution, how many colonies in North America attempted to gain independence from the British?
Ans. 13 colonies

Modern Indian History and Contemporary World History

Q-7. By which year had the American colonies established Provincial Congresses to govern themselves?
Ans. 1774

Q-8. Which treaty was signed after the American victory and marked the departure of the British in 1793?
Ans. Treaty of Paris

Q-9. What are the first ten amendments in the American Constitution known as?
Ans. The Bill of Rights

Q-10. In which year was the American Constitution created?
Ans. 1787

Q-11. The convocation of which body led to the start of the French Revolution in 1789?
Ans. Estates-General

Q-12. How many Third Estate members out of 577 signed the Tennis Court oath?
Ans. 576

Q-13. On which day and year did the historic storming of the Bastille occur?
Ans. 14 July 1789

(Image: Storming of the Bastille)

Quiz Time History

Q-14. The famous document of the French Revolution defining rights is called "Declaration of the rights of Man and of the _____".
- Ⓐ Women
- Ⓑ King
- Ⓒ Ruler
- Ⓓ Citizen

Ans. Ⓓ Citizen

Q-15. Name Louis XVI's famous queen.
Ans. Marie Antoinette

Q-16. In which year did the National Assembly abolish monarchy and declare France to be a 'Republic'?
Ans. 1792

Q-17. Which charter in 1838 pushed for universal male suffrage?
Ans. People's Charter

Q-18. What does "laissez faire" translate to in English?
Ans. "Let it be"

Q-19. Which bill in 1832 allowed greater representation of the growing industrial class?
Ans. The Reform Bill

Q-20. The competition between the Tories and the Whigs led to the passing of which bill that limited the working hours for the working class?
Ans. Ten Hours Act

Industrialisation

- English Industrial Revolution: Causes and Impact on Society
- Industrialisation in other countries: USA, Germany, Russia, Japan
- Socialist Industrialisation: Soviet and Chinese

Q-1. Which device created by James Hargreaves allowed production of yarn in larger quantities?
Ans. Spinning Jenny

Q-2. In which year was the power-loom invented?
Ans. 1787

Power-loom

Q-3. Who created the steam engine in the 1760s?
Ans. James Watt

Quiz Time History

Q-4. In which year did Britain organise the world's first industrial fair?
Ans. 1851

Q-5. During the revolution, what replaced charcoal in the iron smelting industry?
Ans; Coke

Q-6. When workers migrated to cities for employment, Manchester was a popular choice. What was this city nicknamed?
Ans. 'Cottonpolis'

Q-7. The Luddites were English _____ workers who were against the changes that the Industrial Revolution brought.
    Ⓐ Coal   Ⓑ Farm
    Ⓒ Textile   Ⓓ Automobile
Ans. Ⓒ Textile

Q-8. In which year was a General Strike organised involving cotton workers that ceased cotton production across Britain?
Ans. 1842

Q-9. Who founded the Slater Mill?
Ans. Samuel Slater

Q-10. Which company in America started the industrialisation of the watch industry in 1854?
Ans. Waltham Watch Company

Q-11. Which businessman famous for bringing industrialisation to America, also has a city in Massachusetts named after him?
Ans. Francis Cabot Lowell

Q-12. What were producer cartels shaped by banks in Germany called?
Ans. Cartels

Modern Indian History and Contemporary World History

Q-13. What was the first German cartel, formed in 1828?
Ans. Neckar Salt Union

Q-14. In which year were serfs emancipated in Russia?
Ans. 1861

Q-15. Which Russian policy maker made the government improve banking tariffs and encouraged investment from the West between 1892 and 1903?
Ans. Sergei Witte

Q-16. In which year was a Ministry of Industry created in Japan to improve economic policy?
Ans. 1870

Q-17. In the Japanese context, what were "zaibatsu"?
- Ⓐ Textile factories
- Ⓑ Business conglomerates
- Ⓒ Small mills
- Ⓓ Landlords

Ans. Ⓑ Business conglomerates

Q-18. The "Gosplan" or State Planning Committee was responsible for the _____ side of the Soviet Union.
- Ⓐ Social
- Ⓑ Artistic
- Ⓒ Economic
- Ⓓ Industrial

Ans. Ⓒ Economic

Q-19. Who enforced Collectivisation in the Soviet Union between 1928 and 1940?
Ans. Stalin

Q-20. In which year did China's first Five Year Plan begin?
Ans. 1953

Nation-State System

- Rise of Nationalism in 19th century
- Nationalism : State-building in Germany and Italy
- Disintegration of Empires Through the Emergence of Nationalities

Q-1. Which national revolution created the first nation-state in Central Europe?
Ans. Serbian Revolution

Q-2. In which year did Belgium gain independence from The Netherlands?
Ans. 1831

Q-3. Who led the revolt in Hungary against Austrian rule?
Ans. Lajos Kossuth

Q-4. In which year was the Congress of Berlin held?
Ans. 1878

Q-5. In which year was Poland absorbed into Russia?
Ans. 1831

Q-6. Which Italian nationalist famously said, "every nation a state; only one state for the entire nation"?
Ans. Giuseppe Mazzini

Q-7. Which revolutionary overthrew the kingdoms of the two Sicilies in 1860?
Ans. Giuseppe Garibaldi

Q-8. In which year did Venetia unify with Italy?
Ans. 1866

Q-9. Before the unification of Germany, Austria and southwestern Germany were predominantly _____.
- **Ⓐ** Catholic
- **Ⓑ** Protestant
- **Ⓒ** Lutheran
- **Ⓓ** Mormon

Ans. **Ⓐ** Catholic

Q-10. Germany was finally unified in 1871, after a war against which nation?
Ans. France

Q-11. Who led Germany into war against Denmark to remove it from Schlesig in 1864?
Ans. Bismarck

Q-12. Which political act of 1867 established the dual monarchy of Austria-Hungary?
Ans. Austro-Hungarian Compromise

Q-13. What was the another name for the Civil Code of 1804?
Ans. Napoleonic Code

Q-14. Which treaty in 1832 recognised Greece as an independent nation?
Ans. Treaty of Constantinople

Q-15. Which Prussian ruler was crowned as the German Emperor in 1871?
Ans. William I

Q-16. What secret society did Giuseppe Mazzini form to take his goals forward?
Ans. Young Italy

Quiz Time History

Giuseppe Mazzini

Q-17. Who was proclaimed the King of united Italy in 1861?
Ans. Victor Emmanuel II

Q-18. In which year did Giuseppe Garibaldi lead the Expedition of the Thousand to South Italy?
Ans. 1860

Q-19. Which place was forcibly incorporated into the United Kingdom in 1801?
Ans. Ireland

Q-20. What name was given to the female figure that became an allegory for the nation in France?
Ans. Marianne

Imperialism and Colonialism
- ❏ Colonial System (Exploitation of New World, Trans-Atlantic Slave Trade, Tribute from Asian Conquests)
- ❏ Types of Empires of Settlement and Non-settlement: Latin America, South Africa, Indonesia, Australia
- ❏ Imperialism and Free Trade: The New Imperialism

Q-1. What plantations did the Portuguese establish off the African coasts that were sustained by slave labour?
- **Ⓐ** Coffee
- **Ⓑ** Sugar
- **Ⓒ** Salt
- **Ⓓ** Fruit

Ans. Ⓑ Sugar

Q-2. What was the "cartaz" system?
Ans. Pass system

Q-3. What system did the Spanish rulers use during the colonisation of America to regulate Native American labour?
Ans. Encomienda System

Q-4. Which Queen funded Columbus's travels?
Ans. Queen Isabella of Castile

Q-5. In which year did the Spanish demand for gold reduce after a place called Potosi began to yield silver?
Ans. 1545

Q-6. What language does the African word for slave trade, or "Maafa" (holocaust) belong to?
Ans. Swahili

Quiz Time History

Q-7. How many eras is the Atlantic slave trade usually divided into?
Ans. Two

Q-8. On which island did the first slaves arrive as part of a labour force?
Ans. Hispaniola

Slave Labour

Q-9. Which country had a monopoly on the African slave trade for more than two hundred years?
Ans. Portugal

Q-10. What was the name given to the trading system, which connected the economies of three continents?
Ans. Triangular Trade

Q-11. What was the most important tribute for the Aztecs?
Ans. Sacrificial victims

Q-12. When the British entered Africa, which place and canal did they want control over?
Ans. South Africa and the Suez Canal

Q-13. Which islands did the Portuguese decide to seize in Indonesia to gain control over the spice trade?
Ans. Maluku or Moluccas islands

Q-14. Who led the Javanese War in 1825 against the Dutch?
Ans. Prince Disponegoro

Q-15. Which disease killed almost 50 percent of the native Australian population in the early years of British colonisation?
Ans. Smallpox

Q-16. What was the grievous economic depression in the United Sates around 1893 called?
Ans. The Panic of 1893

Q-17. The Meiji Restoration was the restoration of imperial rule in which country?
Ans. Japan

Q-18. Which US policy introduced in 1823 disallowed European efforts to colonise land in North or South America?
Ans. The Monroe Doctrine

Q-19. The Second Boer War was fought between the British and the Afrikaans-speaking Dutch settlers of which two Boer republics?
Ans. South African Republic and Orange Free State

Q-20. Which nation fought the First Opium War against the British?
Ans. China

Revolution and Counter-Revolution
- 19th Century European Revolutions
- The Russian Revolution of 1917-1921
- Fascist Counter-Revolution, Italy and Germany
- The Chinese Revolution of 1949

Q-1. Which year was called the 'Year of Revolution' in the 19th century Europe?
Ans. 1848

Q-2. In Prussia, which king agreed to create a new constitution and work towards a united Germany?
Ans. King Frederick William IV

Q-3. In June of 1848, in which city did Austrian military forces clamp down on Czech rebels?
Ans. Prague

Q-4. How many states did the Congress of Vienna establish in Italy?
- **Ⓐ** 10
- **Ⓑ** 13
- **Ⓒ** 9.
- **Ⓓ** 11

Ans. Ⓒ 9

Q-5. Which army helped to finally put down the Hungarian Revolution in 1849?
Ans. Russian

Q-6. In which two months did the coups of the Russian Revolution of 1917 take place?
Ans. February and October

Modern Indian History and Contemporary World History

Q-7. In which year did Nicholas II become the Tzar of Russia?
Ans. 1894

Q-8. In which place did Vladimir Lenin stay in exile during the February Revolution?
Ans. Switzerland

Lenin

Q-9. Which Bolshevik newspaper published Lenin's *April Thesis*?
Ans. *Pravda*

Q-10. What name was given to the new Bolshevik government of which Lenin was the chairman?
Ans. Soviet of the People's Commissars or the SPC

Q-11. Which memorandum in 1921 sent several officers into the Fascist assault groups as leaders?
Ans. Bonomi memorandum

Q-12. Which famous leader led the 'March of Rome'?
Ans. Mussolini

Q-13. Which President appointed Hitler as the Chancellor?
Ans. Hindenberg

Q-14. In which year was the National Socialist German Workers' Party founded?
Ans. 1920

Quiz Time History

Q-15. Which title did Mussolini begin using for himself by 1925?
Ans. II Duce

Q-16. The People's _____ Army was victorious at the end of the Chinese Civil War.
- Ⓐ Liberation
- Ⓑ Free
- Ⓒ National
- Ⓓ Red

Ans. Ⓐ Liberation

Q-17. Who proclaimed the creation of the People's Republic of China in 1949?
Ans. Mao Zedong

Q-18. Which place did Chiang Kai-shek retreat to after the Nationalists defeat in 1949?
Ans. Taiwan

Q-19. What was the name of Peking changed back to after the Communists took it in January 1949?
Ans. Beijing

Q-20. The Battle of Guningtou was fought to win control over which group of islands?
Ans. Kinmen

World Wars
- First and Second World Wars as Total Wars: Societal Implications
- World War I (WWI): Causes and Consequences
- World War II (WWII): Political Consequences

Q-1. Which country mobilised one-quarter of its population for war during WWI?
Ans. Bulgaria

Q-2. In which year did the famous 'Shell Crisis' take place?
Ans. 1915

Q-3. Under which ministry were propaganda agencies unified under in 1918?
Ans. Ministry of Information

Q-4. Which President created the Office of War Information in 1942?
Ans. Roosevelt

Q-5. The assassination of which Archduke became the immediate cause of WW1?
Ans. Franz Ferdinand

Q-6. What "crisis" among the political players of Europe led to WWI in 1914?
Ans. July crisis

Quiz Time History

Q-7. Which of these was not a cause of WWI?
- **Ⓐ** Imperialism
- **Ⓑ** Nationalism
- **Ⓒ** Arms race
- **Ⓓ** Religion

Ans. Ⓓ Religion

Q-8. Which of these nations was not a part of the 'Triple Alliance'?
- **Ⓐ** Italy
- **Ⓑ** Germany
- **Ⓒ** Britain
- **Ⓓ** Austria-Hungary

Ans. Ⓒ Britain

Q-9. On which date was the Treaty of Versailles signed?
Ans. June 28, 1919

Q-10. After the Russian armies were defeated by German and Austrian forces, which treaty did the new communist government sign in 1918?
Ans. Treaty of Brest-Litovsk

Q-11. Which German ruler abdicated the throne after WWI?
Ans. Kaiser Wilhelm II

Q-12. After the end of WWI, which government fell after the Allies occupied Constantinople?
Ans. Ottoman government

Q-13. Which three states did the Soviet Union acquire after WWII?
Ans. Estonia, Latvia and Lithuania

Q-14. Which country annexed Saar, a German state in 1947?
Ans. France

Q-15. Which plan in 1944 suggested removing all industrial war resources from Germany?
Ans. The Morgenthau Plan

Q-16. What was the 'European Recovery Program' better known as?
Ans. Marshall Plan

Q-17. In which year was the European Union founded?
Ans. 1951

European Union Emblem

Q-18. Which new body was created in 1945 to replace the failed League of Nations?
Ans. United Nations

Q-19. How many zones of occupation was Germany split into after WWII?
    Ⓐ 6   Ⓑ 2
    Ⓒ 4   Ⓓ 3
Ans. Ⓒ 4

Q-20. In which year was the independent state of Israel created?
Ans. 1948

Cold War

- Emergence of Two Blocs
- Integration of West Europe and US Strategy; Communist East Europe
- Emergence of Third World and Non-Alignment
- UN and Dispute Resolution

Q-1. What is the full form of NATO?
Ans. North Atlantic Treaty Organisation

Q-2. The Warsaw Pact was a mutual defence treaty between how many Eastern European communist states?
Ans. Eight

Q-3. In which year did Winston Churchill make his famous "Sinews of Peace" address in Westminster College?
Ans. 1946

Q-4. Which two nations signed the Molotov-Ribbentrop Pact?
Ans. Soviet Union and Germany

Q-5. In which year did the Cuban missile crisis occur?
Ans. 1962

Q-6. Which war marked the first military conflict between the West and the Communists?
Ans. The Korean War

Modern Indian History and Contemporary World History

Q-7. Which general did President Truman remove in 1950, fearing the involvement of the United States in an Asian land war?
Ans. General Douglas MacArthur

Q-8. Through which act was the Central Intelligence Agency created?
Ans. National Security Act, 1947

Q-9. Stalin prevented the ____ block nations from receiving aid from the Marshall Plan.
- **Ⓐ Eastern**
- **Ⓑ Western**
- **Ⓒ Central**
- **Ⓓ Left**

Ans. Ⓐ Eastern

Q-10. In the Italian general elections of 1948, which party defeated the Communist-Socialist alliance?
Ans. Christian democrats

Q-11. Bizonia was the combination of German occupation zones belonging to which two countries?
Ans. United States and Britain

Q-12. Which new currency was introduced in Germany to replace the Reichsmark?
Ans. Deutsche Mark

German Currency

Quiz Time History

Q-13. The Berlin Blockade prevented food and supplies from reaching which part of Berlin?
- Ⓐ North
- Ⓑ South
- Ⓒ East
- Ⓓ West

Ans. Ⓓ West

Q-14. The Operation Little Vittles involved dropping _____ to children from aircrafts.
- Ⓐ Food
- Ⓑ Clothes
- Ⓒ Candy
- Ⓓ Toys

Ans. Ⓒ Candy

Q-15. Where was the Non-Aligned Movement founded?
Ans. Belgrade

Q-16. Which famous leader spoke about the purpose of the Non-Aligned Movement during the Havana declaration of 1979?
Ans. Fidel Castro

Q-17. Which of these countries were not among the founding members of the Non-Aligned Movement?
- Ⓐ India
- Ⓑ Ghana
- Ⓒ Indonesia
- Ⓓ Nigeria

Ans. Ⓓ Nigeria

Q-18. How many principle bodies does the United Nations have?
Ans. 6

Q-19. Which group of developing countries had their first meeting in Algiers in 1967 and created the Charter of Algiers?
Ans. Group of 77

Q-20. Who heads the United Nations Secretariat?
Ans. Secretary-General

Colonial Liberation
- Latin America-Bolivar
- Arab World-Egypt
- Africa-Apartheid to Democracy
- South-East Asia-Vietnam

Q-1. In which year was the Venezuelan Declaration of Independence adopted?
Ans. 1811

Q-2. Name the first President of Venezuela.
Ans. Simon Bolivar

Q-3. In which battle in 1819 did Columbia (New Granada) win independence from Spanish monarchy?
Ans. Battle of Boyaca

Q-4. Which treaty created Uruguay as an independent state?
Ans. Treaty of Motevideo

Q-5. Which battle is considered as the last of the Spanish American wars of independence?
Ans. Battle of Ayacucho

Q-6. Who was the first President of the United Arab Republic?
Ans. Gamal Abdel Nasser

Q-7. In which year was the Palestinian Liberation Organisation (PLO) established in Jordon?
Ans. 1964

Q-8. Which movement forced Egyptian King Farouk to abdicate the throne?
Ans. Free Officers Movement

Q-9. The 1967 Arab-Israeli War is also known as the ____ Day War.
- Ⓐ Five
- Ⓑ Six
- Ⓒ Seven
- Ⓓ Eight

Ans. Ⓑ Six

Q-10. The Tripartite Aggression in 1956 involved the nationalisation of which canal?
Ans. Suez Canal

Q-11. In which year was Apartheid introduced as an official policy in South Africa?
Ans. 1948

An Apartheid Poster

Q-12. Which of these was not one of the four racial groups that South Africans were classified into after 1948?
- Ⓐ White
- Ⓑ Coloured
- Ⓒ Asian
- Ⓓ Boer

Ans. Ⓓ Boer

Q-13. In which year was non-white political representation abolished in South Africa?
Ans. 1970

Q-14. How many years did Nelson Mandela spend in prison after his arrest in 1962?
Ans. 27

Q-15. Which South African President began negotiations to stop apartheid in 1990?
Ans. Frederik Willem de Klerk

Q-16. In which year did the first Indo-China war begin?
Ans. 1946

Q-17. Which body fought against the US and South Vietnamese governments during the Vietnam War?
Ans. Viet Congress or National Liberation Front

Q-18. Name the capital of South Vietnam, which was captured, by the National Liberation Front and People's Army in 1975?
Ans. Saigon

Q-19. Which offensive operations began in December 1974 to defeat the government Republic of Vietnam?
Ans. 1975 Spring Offensive

Q-20. Which helicopter operation evacuated several Vietnamese and American civilians from Saigon in 1975?
Ans. Operation Frequent Wind

Decolonisation and Underdevelopment

❑ Decolonisation: Break up of colonial Empires: British, French, Dutch
❑ Factors constraining Development: Latin America, Africa

Q-1. Which was the first country to seek independence from Britain at the end of WWII?
Ans. India

Q-2. Which two British colonies in Africa had gained their independence by 1957?
Ans. Gold Coast and Sudan

Q-3. What did the British Commonwealth change its name to?
Ans. Commonwealth of Nations

Q-4. The sovereignty of which country was handed over from Britain to China in 1997?
Ans. Hong Kong

Q-5. In 1963, which country joined with Malaya, Sabah and Sarawak to form the Federation of Malaysia?
Ans. Singapore

Q-6. Who founded the French Fifth Republic?
Ans. Charles de Gaulle

Q-7. What political body was created to replace the colonial "French Empire"?
Ans. The French Union

Modern Indian History and Contemporary World History

Q-8. In which massacre did French authorities open fire in an Algerian market town in 1945?
Ans. Setif massacre

Q-9. In which year did Algeria gain independence from the French?
Ans. 1962

Q-10. Which crisis during the Algerian War of Independence led to the return of Charles de Gaulle after a period of ten years?
Ans. May 1958 crisis

Q-11. In which year was the Proclamation of Indonesian Independence made?
Ans. 1945

Q-12. Which Indonesian leader was elected as President after the Proclamation of Indonesian Independence?
Ans. Sukarno

Q-13. In 1986 which island was allowed to secede from the Netherlands Antilles federation?
Ans. Aruba

Q-14. What is the full form of ISI, a developmental model used by Latin America?
Ans. Import Substitution Industrialisation

Q-15. Who coined the phrase "Third World"?
Ans. Alfred Sauvy

Q-16. What is the full form of the organisation, IMF that was established in 1944?
Ans. International Monetary Fund

Quiz Time History

Logo of International Monetary Fund (IMF)

Q-17. Who was the UN Secretary-General who died in plane crash when he was on his way to mediate the Congo crisis?
Ans. Dag Hammarskjold

Q-18. In which year did Kenya gain independence?
Ans. 1963

Q-19. Which revolution in the late 1950s is also known as "The Wind of Destruction"?
Ans. The Rwandan Revolution

Q-20. Who became the first Prime Minister of Zimbabwe in 1980?
Ans. Robert Mugabe

Unification of Europe

❏ Post War Foundations: NATO and European Community
❏ Consolidation and Expansion of European Community/European Union

Q-1. How many member nations does NATO have?
Ans. 28

Q-2. Which NATO program is aimed at building trust between NATO and other European and former Soviet states?
Ans. Partnership for Peace

Q-3. The total military budget of all NATO members makes up more than ____ % of the world's defence budget.
    Ⓐ 50   Ⓑ 30
    Ⓒ 90   Ⓓ 70
Ans. Ⓓ 70

Q-4. Who was the first Secretary-General of NATO?
Ans. Lord Ismay

Q-5. What new form of alphabet did NATO introduce?
Ans. NATO phonetic alphabet or NATO spelling alphabet

North Atlantic Treaty Organisation Alphabet

Quiz Time History

Q-6. Name the two supreme commanders of the NATO.
Ans. Supreme Allied Commander Atlantic and Supreme Allied Commander Europe

Q-7. Which was the first major naval project undertaken by the Allied Commander Atlantic?
Ans. Exercise Mainbrace

Q-8. In which year did Exercise Grand Slam take place?
Ans. 1952

Q-9. The NATO Tiger Association was created to promote friendship and solidarity between NATO ____ forces.
- Ⓐ Armed
- Ⓑ Naval
- Ⓒ Air
- Ⓓ Land

Ans. Ⓒ Air

Q-10. Which state made a proposal to join NATO in 1954 and was rejected?
Ans. Soviet Union

Q-11. Which of these nations were not among the six original members of the European Community?
- Ⓐ Belgium
- Ⓑ France
- Ⓒ Switzerland
- Ⓓ Italy

Ans. Ⓒ Switzerland

Q-12. Through which treaty was the European Community subsumed into the European Union?
Ans. Maastricht Treaty

Q-13. How many member states does the European Union (EU) have?
Ans. 27

Q-14. Which Portuguese Prime Minister became the President of the European Commission in 2004?
Ans. Jose Manuel Barroso

Q-15. The European Parliament is elected every ____ years.
   Ⓐ 2   Ⓑ 5
   Ⓒ 3   Ⓓ 4
Ans. Ⓑ 5

Q-16. In which year was the monetary union "eurozone" created?
Ans. 1999

Q-17. Which two nations became European Union members in 2007?
Ans. Romania and Bulgaria

Q-18. Which treaty in 2009 changed many aspects of the European Union?
Ans. Lisbon Treaty

Q-19. How many courts does the judicial branch of the European Union have?
Ans. 3

Q-20. Which country held a European Union membership referendum in 2012?
Ans. Croatia

Soviet Disintegration and the Unipolar World
- Factors in the Collapse of Soviet Communism and the Soviet Union, 1985-1991
- Political Changes in East Europe, 1989-1992
- End of the Cold War and US Ascendancy in the World
- Globalisation

Q-1. In March of which year did Lithuania declare its independence from the Soviet Union?
Ans. 1990

Q-2. How many republics were part of the Soviet Union?
Ans; 15

Q-3. In which year was the USSR formally dissolved?
Ans. 1991

Q-4. In which state did the Revolutions of 1989 begin?
Ans. Poland

Q-5. Who was the first President of the Russian Federation?
Ans. Boris Yeltsin

Q-6. Which two world leaders met at the Malta Summit?
Ans. George H W Bush and Mikhail Gorbachev

Q-7. In which year was the Commonwealth of Independent Sates formed?
Ans. 1991

Q-8. What was the August Coup involving Mikhail Gorbachev more commonly known as?
Ans. 1991 Soviet Coup

Q-9. In 1990, the ____ Congress of the League of Communists of Yugoslavia convened.
    Ⓐ 15th   Ⓑ 5th
    Ⓒ 14th   Ⓓ 10th
Ans. Ⓒ 14th

Q-10. Which Prime Minister took the place of Nikolai Ryzhkov when he resigned as Chairman of the Council of Ministers in 1991?
Ans. Valentin Pavlov

Q-11. Which political movement meaning "restructuring" was associated with Mikhail Gorbachev?
Ans. Peretroika

Q-12. In which place was the Reykjavik Summit of 1986 held?
Ans. Poland

Q-13. What is the full form of START, a bilateral treaty signed in 1991?
Ans. Strategic Arms Reduction Treaty

Q-14. The INF treaty or Intermediate-Range Nuclear Forces Treaty was an agreement between which two nations?
Ans. United States and Soviet Union

Q-15. The Baltic way or Baltic chain was a peaceful political demonstration across which three Baltic States?
Ans. Estonia, Latvia and Lithuania

Quiz Time History

People holding hands in the Baltic Chain

Q-16. In which year was the term "Globalisation" first used?
Ans. 1930

Q-17. In 2000, how many aspects of globalisation did the International Monetary Fund indentify?
Ans. Four

Q-18. What is the full form of FDI?
Ans. Foreign Direct Investment

Q-19. What name does the United Nations give to a country that shows the lowest indicators of socio-economic development?
Ans. LDC or Least Developed Country

Q-20. What is the full form of GATT?
Ans. General Agreement on Tariffs and Trade

General Questions

General Questions

Q-1. What was the historical name of ancient India?
Ans. Bharatvarsha

Q-2. The Indo-gangetic plain showed signs of a Paleolithic Age. True or False?
Ans. False

Q-3. In the Neolithic age, what was the image of an animal or plant as a symbol for a clan of families called?
Ans. Totem

Q-4. Neolithic people lived in houses of burnt bricks. True or False?
Ans. False

Q-5. The Rig Veda contains 1027 hymns. True or False?
Ans. True

Q-6. How many Vedas exist?
Ans. Four

Q-7. How many Puranas exist?
Ans. 18

Q-8. Valmiki authored the Mahabharata. True or False?
Ans. False

Q-9. Who authored Ashtadhyayi, a book on grammar?
Ans. Panini

General Questions

Q-10. Which of the Vedas first mentioned music?
Ans. Samaveda

Q-11. Milindapanho is a Hindu treatise. True or False?
Ans. False

Q-12. Name the oldest Smriti.
Ans. Manusmriti

Q-13. Where was an Ashokan pillar inscribed in Greek and Aramaic found?
Ans. Kandahar

Q-14. Which ancient civilisation is also called the Sindhu-Sarasvati civilisation?
Ans. Indus Valley Civilisation

Q-15. In which year was the Priest-king statue found in Mohenjodaro?
Ans. 1927

Q-16. The Great Bath of the Indus Valley Civilisation was found at Ropar. True or False?
Ans. False

Q-17. The shape of a stupa was always semi-circular. True or False?
Ans. True

Q-18. Name Chandragupta Maurya's spiritual guru.
Ans. Bhadrabahu

Q-19. Name the son of Bindusara.
Ans. Ashoka

Q-20. Who established the Sunga dynasty?
Ans. Pushyamitra Sunga

Quiz Time History

Q-21. Which famous war had a deep impact on Ashoka and led to his conversion to Buddhism?
Ans. Kalinga War

Q-22. How many classes of Mauryan society were mentioned in the Arthashastra?
Ans. Seven

Q-23. Who was the author of *Mani Makalai*?
Ans. Sittlai Satnar

Q-24. Champa was one of the 16 Mahajanapadas. True or False?
Ans. True

Q-25. What was the capital of the Gupta Empire?
Ans. Pataliputra (Patna)

Q-26. Babur introduced Persian painting to India. True or False?
Ans. True

Q-27. Who founded the city of Agra?
Ans. Sikandar Lodi

Q-28. Only non-Muslims had to pay the Zakat tax. True or False?
Ans. False

Q-29. Which Mughal ruler commissioned the Taj Mahal?
Ans. Shah Jahan

Q-30. Who ascended the throne after Babur's death?
Ans. Humayun

Q-31. Who authored *Ain-i-Akbari* and *Akbarnama*?
Ans. Abul Fazl

General Questions

Q-32. The Qutub Minar was built by Qutubuddin Aibak. True or False?
Ans. True

Q-33. Who built the Buland Darwaza?
Ans. Akbar

Q-35. The officers during the Mughal period were called *Mansabdars*. True or False?
Ans. True

Q-36. Which Mughal ruler was responsible for the death of the sixth Sikh guru?
Ans. Jahangir

Q-37. Mumtaz Mahal was Jahangir's wife. True or False?
Ans. False

Q-38. In which year did Guru Nanak establish The Khalsa?
Ans. 1699

Q-39. In which year was Shivaji born?
Ans. 1627

Q-40. Name the two major taxes of the Marathas.
Ans. Chauth and Sardeshmukhi

Q-41. Who fought the Marathas in the Third Battle of Panipat?
Ans. Ahmad Shah Abdali

Q-42. In which year did Abdali take over Delhi?
Ans. 1760

Q-43. Name Akbar's most famous Hindu wife.
Ans. Jodha Bai

Q-44. Who was the sixth Mughal emperor?
Ans. Aurangzeb

Q-45. Which Sikh guru militarised the Sikh religion?
Ans. Guru Gobind Singh

Q-47. Who was the last Lodi Sultan of Delhi?
Ans. Ibrahim Khan Lodi

Q-48. Who established the Sur dynasty?
Ans. Sher Shah Suri

Q-49. In which year was the Battle of Buxar fought?
Ans. 1764

Q-50. In which battle did Nadir Shah defeat the Mughal army in 1739?
Ans. Battle of Karnal

Q-51. For which emperor was the famous Peacock Throne created?
Ans. Shah Jahan

Q-52. Chishti, Suhrawardi and Qadiri are all orders of what movement?
Ans. Sufi movement

Q-53. Name the first Chishti saint.
Ans. Abu Ishaq Shami

Q-54. Which Bhakti saint composed a retelling of the Ramayana in Awadhi?
Ans. Tulsidas

Q-55. Who founded the *Ekasarana Dharma*?
Ans. Srimanta Sankardeva

Q-56. Which revolt is often called India's First War of Independence?
Ans. The revolt of 1857

General Questions

Q-57. Mangal Pandey was a sepoy in the Bengal infantry. True or False?
Ans. True

Q-58. Who was the Governor-General of India during the Revolt of 1857?
Ans. Charles Canning

Q-59. How many times was the Delhi Darbar held?
Ans. Three

Q-60. Who was responsible for the passing of the Bengal Tenancy Bill?
Ans. Lord Dufferin

Q-61. Where is the Victoria Memorial Hall located?
Ans. Calcutta (Kolkata)

Q-62. In which year did the Partition of Bengal take place?
Ans. 1905

Q-63. Who was the Rowlatt Act named after?
Ans. Sidney Rowlatt

Q-64. In which city did the Jallianwala Bagh massacre take place?
Ans. Amritsar

Q-65. In which year was the University of Delhi established?
Ans. 1922

Q-66. Which famous act of 1935 separated Burma from India?
Ans. The Government of India Act

Q-67. The Cripp's Mission came about as an attempt to seek India's cooperation in WWII. True or False?
Ans. True

Q-68. In 1943, a devastating famine struck Bengal. True or False?
Ans. True

Q-69. In which year the Quit India Movement launched?
Ans. 1942

Q-70. Which African state did Gandhiji work in before he begun the fight for Indian Independence?
Ans. South Africa

Q-71. What does "Swaraj" mean?
Ans. Self-rule or self-governance

Q-72. In which year was the Indian National Congress (INC) founded?
Ans. 1885

Q-73. The All India Muslim League was founded in Calcutta. True or False?
Ans. False

Q-74. Which reforms were also known as the Indian Councils Act, 1909?
Ans. The Morley-Minto Reforms

Q-75. In which year was the Gandhi-Irwin Pact signed?
Ans. 1931

Q-76. Who was the first Deputy Prime Minister of India?
Ans. Sardar Vallabhbhai Patel

General Questions

Q-77. Liaquat Ali Khan became the first Prime Minister of Pakistan. True or False?
Ans. True

Q-78. Name the boundary line between India and Pakistan that was announced upon the Partition.
Ans. Radcliffe Line

Q-79. Who painted The *Last Supper*?
Ans. Leonardo da Vinci

Q-80. The Oration on the Dignity of Man is a treatise by Pica della Mirandola. True or False?
Ans. True

Q-81. In which century did the Black Death take millions of live across Europe?
Ans. 14th century

Q-82. Who wrote the *Ninety-Five Theses*?
Ans. Martin Luther

Q-83. Who coined the word "Utopia"?
Ans. Thomas More

Q-84. What famous motto used during the French Revolution was later made the national motto of France?
Ans. Liberty, Equality, Fraternity

Q-85. Before the French Revolution, the society in France was divided into four estates. True or False?
Ans. False

Q-86. In which year did the Continental Congress adopt the Declaration of Independence for America?
Ans. 1776

Quiz Time History

Q-87. The United States Bill of Rights contains 12 amendments. True or False?
Ans. False

Q-88. Around which capital city was the February Revolution in Russia centred?
Ans. Petrograd

Q-89. What name was given to the 1905 massacre in Russia where the Imperial Guard shot down innocent demonstrators?
Ans. Bloody Sunday

Q-90. Name the founding father of the People's Republic of China.
Ans. Mao Zedong

Q-91. In which year was Archduke Franz Ferdinand assassinated?
Ans. 1914

Q-92. The Armistice Day commemorates the armistice signed between the Allies of WWI and Germany. True or False?
Ans. True

Q-93. Which countries comprised the Triple Entente in 1907?
Ans. France, Britain and Russia

Q-94. What was another name for the First Balkan Crisis?
Ans. Bosnian Crisis or the Annexation Crisis

Q-95. Which secret treaty was signed between Otto von Bismarck and Nikolay Girs in 1887?
Ans. The Reinsurance Treaty

General Questions

Q-96. Which two nations fought in the Battle of Tannenberg during WWI?
Ans. Russia and Germany

Q-97. Name the 1917 failed French attack on the Western Front during WWI?
Ans. Nivelle Offensive

Q-98. In which year was the Ottoman-German Alliance established?
Ans. 1914

Q-99. Mussolini was the 40th Prime Minister of Italy. True or False?
Ans. True

Q-100. In which year did Adolf Hitler become the Chancellor of Germany?
Ans. 1933

Q-101. Name Adolf Hitler's autobiography.
Ans. *Mein Kampf*

Q-102. Which nation went to war with Britain in the Battle of Britain in 1940?
Ans. Germany

Q-103. Which famous battle of control took place in 1942 and 1943, between Germany and it's allies against the Soviet Union?
Ans. Battle of Stalingrad

Q-104. Which declaration was a statement summoning the surrender of Japan in WWII?
Ans. Potsdam Declaration

Quiz Time History

Q-105. What were "Little Boy" and "Fat Man" code names for during WWII?
Ans. Atomic bombs dropped over Hiroshima and Nagasaki

Q-106. The failed Bay of Pigs invasion was an attempt to overthrow which leader?
Ans. Fidel Castro

Q-107. The "Space Race" was a competition between which two nations for domination in space exploration?
Ans. United States and Soviet Union (USSR)

Q-108. In which year was the United Nations founded?
Ans. 1945

Author: Vikas Khatri
Format: Paperback
Language: English
Pages: 104
Price: ₹ 96.00

Quiz Time Mathematics aims to sharpen your mathematical and reasoning skills by putting up simple yet interesting questions and quizzes before you to solve them as logically as possible with the help of various mathematical formulae and principles. All the questions and quizzes have been accompanied with answers at the end of each chapter for the readers' convenience.

The book also contains introductory chapters defining explicitly the meaning of mathematics, its innumerable branches, usage and all about the laws, theorems, etc., associated with it. In addition to all these, important mathematical signs, symbols, words, terms, etc. have also been given.

Author: Manasvi Vohra
Format: Paperback
Language: English
Pages: 144
Price: ₹ 110.00

The study of environment is important for us as we are an integral part of the environment. It includes composite physical and biological sciences including subjects, such as Ecology, Botany, Zoology, Physics, Chemistry, Soil Science, Geography, etc. Environmental studies also incorporate human relationships, perceptions and policies towards the environment. Hence, in order to understand and learn more about the environment; and to find answers queries people consider mysteries nature, Environment Quiz Book is an ideal one.

The book includes several interesting and simple:
- Questions & Answers
- MCQs • Fill in the Blanks
- Crossword • Word Search
- True & False

Author: Vikas Khatri
Format: Paperback
Language: English
Pages: 152
Price: ₹ 110.00

- Enjoy mental workouts?
- Like numerical brain teasers?
- Dabble in solving puzzles?
- Use maths occasionally?
- Accept intellectual challenges?
- Love solving riddles?

It "YES" to any of these questions, then this is the right book for you! Also if you want to test your logical skills and also to have fun, then read this collection of brain teasers and check out how smart you are!!

visit our online bookstore: www.vspublishers.com

Author: Rajeev Garg & Amit Garg
Format: Paperback
Language: English
Pages: 192
Price: ₹ 96.00

That is what your child will find in this Science Quiz Book — brilliant ideas brimming with the latest information and simple explanations of fascinating facts and feats about our constantly evolving world.

Designed to boost your child's knowledge base, each page comes alive with new facts in an engrossing form of short Questions and Answers with explanatory illustrations, all of which makes it easy to read, easy to follow and easy to remember.

Author: Ivar Utial
Format: Paperback
Language: English
Pages: 127
Price: ₹ 120.00

Enliven your leisure hours with Quiz Time! It guarantees you to give many hours of exciting mind storming quiz games. Excel your ability to hold social meetings with charisma and quiz gaming. This book employs tested quiz skills in very well-defined structure for easy comprehension. The book is aimed to cater to a large section of the society.

Author: Gladys Ambat
Format: Paperback
Language: English
Pages: 256
Price: ₹ 120.00

Quiz and puzzles are brain fitness fundas of a unique kind! The thrill to win or lose gaming session of a quiz programme can give you an optimum level of mental fitness and alertness. You simply bubble over with the sheer joy of challenge.

The book is a lively presentation for all youngsters and a pleasant leisure companion for the elders. The veteran author has put together over 4000 exciting quizzes and interesting brain-teasers to get you all keyed up. While you race through every page — you could find yourself sitting on the edge of the chair. Yet, you get charged with a spirit of challenge to unearth hidden answers or solve uncharted problems by your latent thinking power.

visit our online bookstore: www.vspublishers.com

Author: Saurabh Aggrwal
Format: Paperback
Language: English
Pages: 256
Price: ₹ 200.00

Author: Dr. Nivedita Ganguli
Format: Paperback
Language: English
Pages: 108
Price: ₹ 96.00

Author: V. Rajesh
Format: Paperback
Language: English
Pages: 104
Price: ₹ 120.00

Did you know that crossword puzzles first appeared in the New York World in 1913, and soon became a popular feature in newspapers? Did you know that Kellog's as a brand had spent $90,000 on advertising, more than 100 years ago in 1906, including one $4000 a page ad in the Ladies Home Journal. Apple had lured John Sculley away from Pepsi because they wanted him to apply his marketing skills to the personal computer market and not on fizz drinks. Find facts and trivia from the world of business that will amaze and delight you. The questions in this book have been framed in a way that they are: guessable with intelligent, lateral thinking; interesting, amusing, and surprising.

Do you feel that life sometimes pulls you down? Do you keep on searching for some light to pull you out of darkness? Do you feel so wrapped up in your own issues that you miss out the real treasures of life? Probably this book may create a full-stop to your search. The episodes present in the book would enable you to see life from a brighter perspective. The 'In a Nutshell' portion following each episode would give direction towards Life Management. Quotations present in form of 'Food for Thought' would give rich nutrition to your thought process. Our wrong perspective towards everyday issues makes life more complicated. Changing perspective would enable us to live life fully.

It is easy to skip a question during an exam if it is "Out of Syllabus" but what do you do when faced with a situation in life for which you were not given any input? Can you run away from the situation hiding behind the "Out of Syllabus" excuse?

Career is one area where one is expected to know and manage contingencies. After all a person is paid to handle things and deliver results. The reality is that most people get a lot of academic and conceptual inputs relating to one's career choice but very little practical inputs on how to effectively use the academic learning.

visit our online bookstore: www.vspublishers.com

Also available in Hindi, Bangla, Tamil	Also available in Hindi	Also available in Hindi
Author: Dr. C.L. Garg/ Amit Garg	Author: Vikas Khatri	Author: Ivar Utial
Format: Paperback	Format: Paperback	Format: Paperback
Language: English	Language: English	Language: English
Pages: 120	Pages: 160	Pages: 120
Price: ₹ 140.00	Price: ₹ 150.00	Price: ₹ 96.00

Science projects and models play a pivotal role in inculcating scientific temper in young minds and in harnessing their skills. school students of senior classes have to work on such projects and these carry much weight in their overall performance.

All these aspects have been considered during the compilation of the projects and models. This book will also be an ideal choice for parents interested in enhancing scientific temper of their children; and for hobbyists.

The book has 81 Classroom projects on: Physics, Chemistry, Biology & Electronics for Sec. & Sr. Sec. Students

A study of Science and Scientific theories is almost incomplete without relevant and methodical Experiments. In fact, experiments are an inseparable part of any scientific study or research. In this book, the author has tried to simplify science to the readers, particularly the school-going students, through easy and interesting experiments. The experiments given in the book are based on one scientific phenomena or another, such as atmospheric pressure, high and low temperatures, boiling, freezing and melting points of solids, liquids, gases, gravitational force, magnetism, electricity, solubility of substances, etc.

Supplementary science books not only interest and excite young students, but also stimulate their interest in the subject.

This exciting book shows you how to have fun with 101 Science Games. There is little doubt that science experiments can be quite interesting and useful in discovering mysteries of nature.

The book is fully illustrated with step-by-step instructions to give you first hand experience of making simple scientific equipments like :
Telescope
Barometer
Hectometer
Model Electric Motor
Electroscope
Periscope
Steam Turbine; and more…

visit our online bookstore: www.vspublishers.com

Also available in Hindi

Author: Vikas Khatri
Format: Paperback
Language: English
Pages: 120
Price: ₹ 100.00

Author: Prosenjit Saha
Format: Paperback
Language: English
Pages: 108
Price: ₹ 295.00

Author: A.H. Hashmi
Format: Paperback
Language: English
Pages: 122
Price: ₹ 150.00

54 cool and Challenging art working, projects, crafts, experiments and more for kids!!!

Unplugging kids from their MP3 players and game systems for one-on-one family time is a great way to reconnect in today's hectic world. And what better way to spend time together than doing an activity that's not only fun but also promotes creativity and self-expression?

Greatest Crafts and Projects for Children is packed with 54 craft projects ranging from outdoor projects to gifts and party favours to holiday decor to projects that promote learning through play with step-by-step instructions to guide children to successful completion of each project.

We believe everyone can draw or paint. Of course some people are naturally talented but we are all capable of channelling our artistic skills and creativity.

With this belief in mind, we have published this Drawing and Painting Course Volume II for children who want to learn and master the art in a fun way. This book starts with the basics – lines, shades, texture, balance, harmony, rhythm, tone, colours, etc., and goes on to teach the various different techniques of drawing and painting with step-by-step instructions, accompanied by an audio-visual CD.

Children have always been attracted towards bright colours, various shapes and diverse objects that they see around them. Nature fascinates them. The beautiful birds, animals, flowers and trees fire their imagination and they want to capture it on paper. But how, for all are not artists by birth.

Well, this book has been especially developed for those who want to learn and master the art in a fun way. The step-by-step instructions, along with the audio-visual CD, will show you how to create beautiful pictures. See how a circle or an oval transforms into a flower or a peacock; a few lines here, and a few there become a human figure.

visit our online bookstore: www.vspublishers.com

www.ingramcontent.com/pod-product-compliance
Lightning Source LLC
Chambersburg PA
CBHW070331230426
43663CB00011B/2284